WINDOW *of the* SOUL

WINDOW
of the SOUL

The Kabbalah of Rabbi Isaac Luria
(1534–1572)

Selections from Chayyim Vital

Translated by Nathan Snyder
Edited and with an introduction
by James David Dunn

WEISER BOOKS
San Francisco, CA / Newburyport, MA

First published in 2008 by
Red Wheel/Weiser, LLC
With offices at:
500 Third Street, Suite 230
San Francisco, CA 94107
www.redwheelweiser.com

Library of Congress Cataloging-in-Publication Data
Vital, Hayyim ben Joseph, 1542 or 3-1620.
['Ets hayim. English. Selections]
Window of the soul : the kabbalah of Rabbi Isaac Luria (1534–1572) :
selections from Chayyim Vital / translated by Nathan Snyder ; edited and
with an introduction by James David Dunn.
p. cm.
Includes bibliographical references.
ISBN 978-1-57863-428-6 (alk. paper)
1. Cabala—Early works to 1800. I. Luria, Isaac ben Solomon, 1534–1572.
II. Dunn, James David. III. Snyder, Nathan. IV. Title.
BM525.V52113 2008
296.1'6—dc22
2007033034

Cover and text design by Jessica Dacher.
Typeset in Goudy.
Cover illustration © helloyiyin/iStockphoto.com.

Printed in the United States of America
MV
10 9 8 7 6 5 4 3 2 1

The paper used in this publication meets the minimum requirements of the
American National Standard for Information Sciences—Permanence of Paper
for Printed Library Materials Z39.48-1992 (R1997).

In memory of Rabbi Ben-Zakkai

The wolf also shall dwell with the lamb,
and the leopard shall lie down with the kid;
and the calf and the young lion and the fatling
together; and a little child will lead them.
(Is., XII)

To all people who struggle with God.

Contents

Foreword

This book is the result of four years of extremely intensive research into all the available academic studies that touched upon the teachings of Luria, as well as a line-by-line exposition of the original texts of the *Etz Hayyim* and other sources. The result of this dedicated scholarship is a comprehensive selection from the teachings of Isaac Luria that gives clarity to his conceptual system.

For Prof. Dunn and Nathan Snyder to have created a selection of the teachings of Rabbi Isaac Luria as preserved in the *Etz Hayyim* and to have translated them from their Hebrew original into English is, in itself, a spiritually audacious undertaking. It is even more impressive for having been done by two people with great respect for and commitment to the rigorous academic learning of Judaism in all its manifestations.

Not everyone is ready to concede the relevance of mystical traditions in the modern world. This requires personal detachment, objectivity, and a neutral stance—to the degree that they are possible. But when the spirit of God irrupts into one's soul, it is a wondrous occurrence that reason can neither contemplate nor hope to understand. The great medieval Jewish philosopher Moses Maimonides understood this. Likewise, the towering 20th-century theologian Abraham Joshua Heschel taught that the true spirit of Judaism can only be probed when we are personally open and responsive to the divine Voice that comes from on-high.

The mystics of all religions break loose from the narrow limitations of human reason and the constraints of denotative language. They search instead for an evocative language that can express their higher spiritual visions. They hope that those who have similar religious experiences will find some solace and guidance in their written testimonies. Yet only Providence can determine who will have the spiritual capacity and sensitivity to understand their teachings and the determination and commitment to make them accessible to others.

Prof. Dunn's personal fascination with the teachings of Luria has led him to probe the depths of those teachings in an effort to better understand their infinite complexities and make them accessible to the general English-speaking public. He found, in Nathan Snyder, someone who understood his own profound calling—someone equally committed to exploring Luria's work and bringing this precious jewel to light.

Dunn's introduction to the selection is an essential primer for any serious reader who yearns to encounter first-hand the teachings of Luria. A few, but very sharp and pointed, remarks help to frame Dunn's study and and prepare his readers. Dunn explains that "the greater part of Isaac Luria's cosmogony unfolds in nonmaterial realms, long before creation itself and the world as we know it." He expands on this, saying: "The history of humanity's innermost worlds is far older than the present creation and its ontology." In other words, we should not forget that what is of primary concern to Luria is the spiritual pre-history of the human soul, the roots of which lie in realms higher than the physical universe. These roots are antecedent to the creation of our entire universe in all ways. Thus—and this is of crucial importance to Dunn—the ultimate quest is not a vain intellectual pursuit of abstractions, but an intense search for self-transcendence through ethical self-scrutiny and commitment to a life of piety.

We must prepare ourselves ethically and spiritually before undertaking the reading of Luria if we are to glean its riches. We cannot remain personally impervious to its impact if we understand its religious import. Understanding Luria means being transformed in our lives. If we are not transformed, we have not truly "read" him. We do not simply have "a book" in our hands, and "reading," in this case, is much more than a rational enterprise. Our intuition must be activated to the fullest before we embark on the journey. If our souls are not already aflame when we open the first page and turn to the first word, we will encounter only the outer husks of Luria's teaching. This is why this work represents *a meta-academic pursuit*, one that places us in *a Heavenly Academy* where we experience a higher Teaching, a higher Torah.

For Prof. Dunn, kabbalah is the most compressed form of Torah, and the teachings of Luria the most compressed expression of kabbalah. All of Luria's teachings are pervaded with a most vivid imagery that is infinitely complex and infinitely refracted. That is, each set of organic metaphors—and there are many in his teachings—echoes another. They are arranged, as it were, like infinite mirrors (and windows) that face each other. From the highest to the lowest levels of reality, events occur and recur—in the Heavens and on the Earth—in a constant effort to repair the Universe created by God and bring unity to the Divine Creator.

Dunn explains that the first well-known concept in Luria's mystical system, *tsimtsum*, is "not only the first creative act to form the pre-All, but it stretches to this very moment as the mystical dialectic that alternates between the transcendental (divine) and the vulgar self." "*Tsimtsum*," he tells us, "is far more than a discrete and static event whereby the Godhead contracted and withdrew itself in order to make a void in which to create. It is an eternally repeating event that connects the Godhead with every creature during the evolving progression of a divine creative moment. . . . *Tsimtsum* is the systolic-diastolic pulse of the Ineffable that changed and exiled Itself, disrupted the harmony of the absolute, and continues to do so at each moment as It creates into this very ontological moment." Thus, in a concise and lucid way, Dunn takes us beyond the conventional understanding of *tsimtsum*.

A significant feature of this work is Dunn's ordering of Luria's teachings into four sections that represent the four letters of the Tetragrammaton (*Yod-Hey-Vav-Hey*):

I.   The Kings of Edom
II. Divine Rebirth
III. Adam among the Worlds
IV. Benedictions of the Soul

This organization hints at the fact that all the processes expounded in Luria's work are events that take place within God as He moves into creation.

To quote Prof. Dunn:

Our book has four central movements (4 chapters) that correspond to YHVH, the Tetragrammaton. It describes the dramatic progression from God into Creation, as He picks up the pieces along the way at each level. God moves from the most subtle and most holy (tip of the Yod, Kings of Edom), progresses downwardly into Creation, but vessels shatter. He continues to rebirth Himself (Hey), creates holy faces and Adam. God works within these faces and Adam. But Adam shatters the vessels again, thereby mixing souls with matter (Vav, World of Creation). The *Shekhinah* goes down to death and is trapped in matter. What remains are fallen worlds immersed in evil and matter. The ultimate moral imperative is for upper worlds, *Ze'ir Anpin* and *Nukva* to work with Adam and mankind so that they might raise these sacred shattered pieces to God, thereby rejoining *Shekhinah* with God again. The final Hey of the Tetragrammaton acts within matter as Adam's children save the worlds and even God Himself.

As Morris Faierstein remarked in his review of the first edition of this book, the four sections also cover the two other central motifs of Lurianic kabbalah: *shevira* (the breaking of the vessels) and *tikkun* (repair of the worlds).

The impressive and erudite work of Nathan Snyder provides a key that opens the doors of the Lurianic corpus to Prof. Dunn. Snyder's great mastery of the Hebrew language, as well as his extensive and deep understanding of Jewish classical sources, are providentially joined—in time, in space, and in spirit—to Prof. Dunn's vision for this book, allowing them together to make a very significant contribution to the field Lurianic kabbalah.

It has been a privilege for me to come to know both Mr. Snyder and Prof. Dunn. It is my hope that you will find in these pages some of the same enlightenment that I have found here.

Rabbi Ernesto V. Yattah

Rabbi Ernesto V. Yattah serves as the rabbi of *Centro Comunitario Chalom*, a Sephardic synagogue in Buenos Aires, Argentina. He previously served as a rabbi at *Congregation Beth Yeshurun* in Houston, Texas (1989–1998).

Preface

In this book, I offer the first selection of kabbalah from the teachings of Rabbi Isaac Luria (1534–1572) translated from the original passages of Hebrew. This book fulfills the need to bring a selection of Isaac Luria's teachings to Judaic and cross-cultural channels in modern society for the first time. The Lurianic texts present an intimidating vast sea of astounding complexity and power that can only be appreciated in original or in translation.

I have attempted to select passages that are universal and stand alone in transcendental value, while staying within the context of Rabbi Luria's teachings. Passages should be read intuitively, along a timeless base. Normative, contemporary communications rarely apply within them.

Luria's kabbalah is as radical as it is revolutionary, because in ways that other kabbalists never thought possible, he answered not only the Jewish people's deepest questions of exile and homelessness, but with a vision given only to the most gifted of kabbalistic mystics, he explained the very structure of the inner worlds of the spirit and of their evolution that led to the ultimate birth of souls and of our cosmos.

We are especially thankful to Yechiel Bar Lev for recognizing the importance of such a work as this and for helping us to publish it.

Rabbi Luria disclosed his revelations of kabbalah to his students some 400 years ago. His message to our present age is past due. Mr. Snyder and I hope that you will find his teachings illuminating, meaningful, and religiously powerful.

Introduction: The Second Adam and the History of Souls

Albert Einstein looked up at the great display of a clear night sky while walking with a friend and exclaimed: "Two things inspire me to awe—the starry heavens above and the moral universe within." I'm sure his friend was not quite prepared to respond to such a lofty and compellingly deep statement. No doubt the world with its many distractions and needs bent the direction of his thoughts earthward again and he put his wonderment of the universes above and within aside. But others have pursued this question with the same unrelenting introspection as Albert Einstein pursued his questions about the universe. And somehow, although their universes are not the same, these thinkers and their mediums are connected masterfully.

Some 400 years before Albert Einstein proposed his Theory of Relativity of the outer universe to the scientific community, a Rabbi named Isaac Luria disclosed his theory of the inner universe and its evolution within the mind of the Ineffable to his students. Luria's theory, which followed the profound suffering and alienation of the Jewish people when they were driven from Spain in 1492, was the greatest growth and transformation ever known to kabbalistic mysticism. And although these events can not necessarily be proven to be connected, no one should doubt the impact that this historical atrocity had upon the minds of the Jewish people in the generations that followed.[1] Seventy-seven years after the Exile, in a small Jewish settlement in upper Galilee called Safed, Isaac Luria not only answered the Jewish people's deepest questions about exile and homelessness, but, with a vision given only to the most gifted of kabbalistic mystics, he explained the very structure of the inner worlds of the spirit and of their evolution that led to the ultimate birth of our cosmos. *It is this evolution that reflects the origin and history of souls, according to the teachings of Rabbi Luria.*

Isaac Luria taught his students orally and left little authentic written material behind. His works were recorded by his students, Joseph ibn Tabul and especially Hayyim Vital. Luria's gift of vision became so acute that, in the year before his death, he confessed that he could read people's souls. Hayyim Vital writes:

> On *Rosh Hodesh Adar* in the year 1571, he told me that he began to attain his comprehension [reading souls] when he was in Egypt. There, he was told to come to

the city of Safed, because I, Hayyim, was living there, in order to teach me. He also told me that he was not required to teach any person other than myself and when I will have learned there will be no reason for him to remain in this world.

He told me that the essence of my Soul was on a higher plane than numerous very exalted angels and I would be able to ascend with my Soul, by means of my deeds, higher than the firmament of the Seventh Heaven.[2]

The greatest part of Isaac Luria's cosmogony unfolds in non-material realms, long before Creation itself and the world as we know it. It moves from the absolute (*en sof*) to a primal space (*tehiru*) in God's own experience, which contains his infinite reflections during each moment of Creation and at every level of reality of all worlds, and finally moves to the most unbalanced sanctum within this space, which comprises the material world and its attendant attributes as we know it today (*klippoth*). The drama of Creation is a *religio*-psychic odyssey nested in God's *very self:* It begins with unity and connected harmony, nonmaterial fullness, total self-possession and inwardness and concludes with the ontological present-ness of today: plurality, disunity, distraction in matter, and dispossessed selves in external worlds of exile.

His cosmogony is truly an open-ended one, because the Creation is a work-in-progress toward restitution (*tikkun*), whereby all subjects of Creation work to return things to their proper place so that Creation's original plan can continue.[3] The world continues in the midst of a breach or interruption of the Creator's original intention and mankind must help to bring things right again, since the true world drama of Creation is *on hold*. According to Isaac Luria and his school, God did not choose to make the world as we know it. But through successive crises in the Godhead caused by imperfection inherent in the nature of Creation, all phenomena devolved to a continually emerging struggle between unity (transcendental inner self) and chaos in matter (corporeal beings). The radical fidelity of *tikkun*—each creature's contemplation of heart and works—and its applications of power upon the inner universes of Creation through successive lifetimes with God will return *His* image (*Shekhinah*) to *Her* true place in unity with God again. The eternal Sabbath will be regained and the realm of matter will be abandoned.

Events are intra-godly images that project onto a dimensionless scale. They lie far beyond common existence in a higher objective reality. Characters are neither male nor female. This duality takes form only after events degenerate to the fall of Adam during Luria's last act of creation.[4]

Isaac Luria taught creation under three central themes—*tsimtsum* (contraction), *shebirath ha-kelim* (breaking of the vessels) and *tikkun* (repair)—but it is *tikkun* that embodies the essence of his entire teaching. *Tsimtsum* is the idea that God withdrew

upon himself or shrank himself to make a void in which to create. Breaking of the vessels is the event that dramatizes the dis-
continuity or imperfection that necessarily exists between the
Creator and created in such a void, yet binds them together
with the moral imperative that has one supra-ultimate conclusion: *tikkun*. Creation must be flawed because, if that which
was created were perfect, then it would be the Godhead itself.
Hence Adam Kadmon, the first archetypical God-humanity,
created in the void outside of the absolute, must necessarily
be imperfect and yet must also reflect the fullest image of the
Divine One. Breaking of the vessels brought catastrophe and
discord into the void (*tehiru*)—a place that no longer contains
the Godhead's full presence and that lies outside of his full
control. Since the Godhead created Adam Kadmon, it also
caused the very imperfection in him that led to his failure.
The same follows for Adam as well. Every creature bears the
mark of its inheritance from Creation and, therefore, from
God himself.[5]

Imperfection and evil are a byproduct of creation at the hands
of the Perfect Creator: blame can fall on neither the Creator
nor the creature, but on the innocence of becoming that
separates them profoundly: It is *Creation itself*. *Tikkun* is their
re-connection. It is the mystical medium that binds the old
harmony with its fallen creatures. The sacred sheen that fell
with Adam and saturated lower worlds joins again with God
through the good acts of his own blind (outer world) but illuminated (inner potentialities) creatures. The divine sparks can

be redeemed through ethical and religious deeds.[6] The present world continues as part of this process and the Creator's most profound imperative—*tikkun*—is that deepest (and still unfulfilled) longing that wells in mankind's very core and has done so even before the twilight of his birth.

The history of humanity's innermost worlds is far older than the present Creation and its ontology. Its medium lies beyond its concerns in the worlds of *sefirot* (divine emanations). It is within these worlds that Isaac Luria and his students describe the inner history of mankind's soul. C. G. Jung's *tiefenpsychologie* confirmed what had already been known among the kabbalists for centuries: ". . . the soul possesses a historical taxonomy and its oldest hierarchies lie in the subconscious mind."[7] Yehuda Liebes rightly points out that academic methodology has tended to bypass

> . . . [this] critical phase of the development of his system . . . the part that touches the soul. The rest of the Ari's [Luria's] ontological teaching served as a mere introduction to this matter, which has not been properly recognized by previous scholars. The reason why they did not . . . is because they did not stop to ask themselves what might have been the *religious* interest that is reflected in the Ari's writings. Instead they looked for answers for abstract issues in Lurianic Kabbala, issues defined a priori as those presumed to be the most important.[8]

Tsimtsum

Tsimtsum (concentration, folding in) is probably one of the most powerful ideas ever to be taught in kabbalistic mysticism. Even to this day, it is unlikely that it has been understood fully enough to be absorbed into the modes of thought of this age because its sheer otherworldliness and multilateral meaning are too difficult and refractory for the modern mind to absorb: If *tsimtsum* is to be understood—*fully understood*—it must be lived each day while the mind is focused inwardly and mystically while looking away from the world and its externalia. The act of *tsimtsum* is not only the first creative act to form the pre-All, but it stretches to this very moment as the mystical dialectic that alternates between the transcendental (divine) and vulgar self.

The roots of potentiality that make up the essence of God rested in the transcendental and dimensionless expanse of *en sof*. Even the metaphysical origins of evil—the roots of judgment and powers of severity (*din*)—lay in full harmony and balance within these eternities: preexistent, latent and yet gravid with the pervasive harmony of *en sof*:

And behold this enigma is very deep. It almost endangers the person who examines it carefully. The upper light diffuses eternally. This light that radiates eternally is called *en sof*. It cannot be grasped in thought nor principal. It is abstracted and separated from all thought and it existed before all that was ever emanated or created.[9]

God sent a beam of light, like a thin ray, from *en sof* into the *tehiru*. This light developed into the first divine being of the *tehiru*—Adam Kadmon.

> And by way of this line there continues and spreads the light of *en sof* beneath. And in that empty space, he emanated, created and made the entirety of all the worlds. And this line, like one thin pipe, in which it spreads and continues, from the seas of the upper light of *en sof*, to the worlds, which are in the place of higher realms and that void.[10]

But this light does not just spread and continue throughout the worlds; it must withdraw itself again if these worlds are to continue their existence. This pulse forms the fabric of Creation and the physiology of sefirotic worlds described in Vital's *Etz Hayyim*. *Tsimtsum is far more than a discrete and static event whereby the Godhead contracted and withdrew itself in order to make a void in which to create: It is an eternally repeating event that connects the Godhead with every creature during the evolving progression of a divine creative moment.* "The upper light moves to lower worlds, then departs, thereby leaving a closing impression upon them."[11] The Ineffable participates fully and fluently with divine pervasiveness. It moves from the light of *en sof* into the inner worlds at every level and, if harmony is broken, it flows back again. Eliahu Klein sums up emanations as ". . . the process of light in two stages. Inner light descends. Enveloping light ascends."[12] In one instant, the primal space is filled with divine intention and living presence (*pleroma*); in the next instant, it withdraws and leaves it as an abyss once more—only slightly different, because it has been changed by the impression that had filled it previously. God's eternal act of creation begins from this point onward: God creates *into* the *tehiru* by filling it with divine emanations and active intelligence, and then withdraws these potentialities again, since Creation can only be possible without the total presence of God (otherwise, the *tehiru* would return to *en sof* again). Everything in the *tehiru* carries influences of double motion of the continually self-renewing *tsimtsum*. According to Isaac Luria, it is this dynamic exchange, and the progressive results of its eternally changing moment of the personality of God among the inner universes of every creature that will ultimately reunite with Creation or efface and separate the powers of *din* that pervade in *tehiru* and thereby rejoin Creator with created.

Tsimtsum is the systolic-diastolic pulse of the Ineffable that changed and exiled itself, disrupted the harmony of the absolute, and continues to do so at each moment as it creates into this very ontological moment.[13]

Creation and Din

Din—the judging power—is that most vital element that has made (and continues to make in each moment of *tsimtsum*)

Creation possible. By its very nature, it is also the foundation for the potentiality of all evil in the world. According to kabbalistic teaching, the truest meaning of judgment is to *set limits*. *Tsimtsum* is an act of limitation and self-determination in the Divine One. And so in Its own act to create, It limits Itself (*din*), and, if one takes the meaning of creature to be a limited being, God becomes as a creature in order to participate in Creation. Not only does the Godhead limit Itself, but every creature must necessarily be inferior to its *tsimtsum*-limited Creator. "The body of Elohim descends at times into the worlds. . . . It is adorned and dressed in clothes [vessels] to coquette in front of her husband and it says: 'See what I do and the developments that I have made!'"[14] Rilke expressed this transcendent meaning inimitably:

Angel, to *you* I will show it, *there!* in your endless vision it stands now, finally upright, rescued at last. . . . Wasn't all this a miracle? Be astounded, Angel, because we *are* this, O Great One . . . we have not failed to make use of these generous spaces, these spaces of *ours*. (How tremendously deep they must be—the millenia do not yet make them overflow with our feelings.)[15]

As imperfect subjects of creation, all bear the weight of *din* and its potential for imbalance and severity during existence. In a deep sense, the potential of all evil is based on *din* and lies hidden in the act of *tsimtsum* itself. But just as much as *din* lies at the root of imperfection and ultimate suffering with evil in the material world, it must also be the saving grace. God created the world that sustains itself through *strict law—din—*and, seeing that it could not exist under this severity alone, God balanced it by including *chessed* (grace and love) in Creation. To live under strict limits, self-determination, and sacrifice while balanced with love opens the path to reconciliation with God (*tikkun*).

There is an even deeper meaning behind God's self-negation and exile in the act of *tsimtsum*. The Divine One limits Itself to create during a divine moment and, during this interval, It becomes less perfect for a more perfect good. It gives of itself (god-*less*) and thereby becomes more god-*full*: God's ever-sacrificing and exiled presence is shared with the innermost being of each creature, and sustains each moment in its self-determined fullness as part of the mystical progression in the greater good of creation.

The Divine One exiles itself to touch its exiled creatures. Isaac Luria and his students understood the ineffable connection between Creator and created: a transcendent kinship of God with God-humanity, entangled in spiritual struggle, evolving toward mutual reabsorbtion of each into the other. And long before the cosmos and light of day, deep in the primal space of the pre-All, these intra-godly experiences formed the most profound tendencies of the structure of souls. The corridors of the soul lead through exile, alienation, and suffering, with self-sacrificing, unfulfilled longing toward reunion and repair (*tikkun*). The fallen God, this lost and elusive presence, will finally rejoin the Father, illumined. Marie-Louise von Franz, a student of C. G. Jung, cites the following passage, attributed to Thomas Aquinas quoting Senior in *Aurora Consurgens*: "There is one that never dies because it sustains itself in steady increase, when the body will be transfigured in the final resurrection of the dead . . . then the *second Adam* will say to the *first Adam* and to his [children]: 'Come, O you blessed ones of my Father.'"[16]

According to Luria, every creature feels the *absence*, emptiness and mark of imperfection that must necessarily be handed on to it. The ultimate calling in this lifetime or in future lifetimes is to re-harmonize (and hence *remove*) inherent imperfections through proper heart and works among all creatures (*tikkun*). But such an existential calling is not easily heard. To pass through old doors to the inner self brings on the symptomology of ancient malaise of the soul.[17] One has only to press on through the density and lassitude of existence and to hope.

The roots of judgment and powers of severity (*din*) were invisible and latent in *en sof*, simply because they were unnecessary in the absolute totality of God's presence. In *tehiru*, however, *din* no longer rests in harmony nor in balance: *tehiru* is a place where God is no longer totally present and where severity and judgment destabilize and devolve to evil whenever their potential is externalized (breaking of the vessels).

The Worlds of Sefirot

In kabbalistic teaching, a *sefira*—plural *sefirot*—is any of the ten potentialities or emanations through which the Divine One manifests its existence in each moment. *Din* is merely one of these potentialities.

> The active God appears as the dynamic unity of the *sefiroth*. . . . The *sefiroth* are the potentialities in which the active God is constituted and in which he achieves his face. . . . The hidden face of God "*anpin penima*" is the interceding moment of life of God that faces us but in spite of all its hiddenness still takes form. His life is expressed on ten levels, each of which absconds and discloses. It streams outwardly and animates creation but at the same time it remains profoundly within and the secret rhythm of his moment, his pulses, is the law of motion of [every] creature.[18]

Kabbalists experience the *sefirot* world as the one true world and as a mystical body that is superimposed upon the external world. The inner life of all creatures, born and unborn, flourished at one time within Adam Kadmon, but now, for all who exist in the blind medium of the present, it lives banished to the most profound depth of each self, in the inner world of one's most hidden being.[19] The entire *sefirot* world is contained in each such inner world and its life is experienced in

Adam Kadmon. Creation forms a *corpus mysticum* in the material and kadmonic worlds. The key element that superfuses
this oneness in the *sefirot* world is the tenth *sefira* (*Shekhinah* or
malkhut). It is as radical as it is remarkable because, without it,
not a single moment of creation would be possible. The tenth
sefira is the most humble and lowest of all of the *sefirot*. *Malkhut*
was "the tail to the lions at the end of Atsilut. . . . Afterward
it descended . . . and is the head of foxes. . . . Her feet go down
to death . . . there among the shells. . . . Sparse light comes to
her. . . ."[20] She is a poor and disabled figure consigned to darkness, dependent upon higher radiance for strength and sur-
vival and trapped in *Kelipa Nogah* (realm of matter). Her upper
aspect is *bina*, the active feminine element that creates among
the worlds. *Malkhut* does not have discernibly divine qualities
like the other nine *sefirot* (e.g., will, wisdom, insight, love,
etc.), but it somehow has the same hidden qualities of *en sof*
itself. It possesses nothing but yet has everything. It receives
the qualities of the other nine *sefirot*, and from the depth of
its mystery, it shares with all who live within its sovereignty.
It yields and retreats, yet touches every living creature. It is
the *eternally effeminate*, the displaced and active God in the
world. *Shebirath ha-kelim* damaged the *Shekhinah* and separated
her from her counterpart, *Ze'ir Anpin* (creative powers). This
separation symbolizes the guilt and the rift between the outer
and inner worlds. *Shekhinah* and *Ze'ir Anpin* were merged in
perfect radiance in the inner worlds of the Godhead until the
rift. *Malkhut* is like a murky gem. *It is a window pane of lapis
specularis that has no brightness (ispaklarya de-lo nahara.) It is
poor compared to the other sefirot because it only receives light and,*

unlike the other sefirot, can not retain the light's own impression within itself.[21]

Creation and this world have been diverted to a new channel for the moment, and until the *Shekhinah* rejoins with her counterpart again, full and fluent Creation can not move through all worlds as before. The *sefira yesod* delivers light and abundance to *malkhut* from the upper *sefirot*. The *Shekhinah* represents the place of the psyche as well as God's active presence everywhere. It is the hidden (yet disclosing) image of God. The unfolding of God is called "He" in the most hidden of his manifestations when he is about to give himself a push toward creation as it were. . . . God, who, in the total unfolding of his being, grace and love, who is attainable at the bottom of our hearts, and thus to whom we can speak, is called "You." But God, in the most extreme of his manifestations, in those circumstances where the totality of his being is affected again in the final and most comprehensive of his attributes, is called "I." This is the level of the real individuation in which God says "I" as a person to himself. . . . This "I" of God is [according to the Kabbalists] one of the most important and deepest teachings—the *Shekhina* —the present and immanent God of all of Creation. [22]

Adam Kadmon and the First Breaking of the Vessels

Sefirot are vessels for the light of *en sof*, which is in them. They are like the garments for the light of *en sof* and form the external shapes (vessels) of this light that gives specific characteristics to each divine emanation when light spreads to the lower worlds. The light of *en sof* forms the light of Adam Kadmon and he is the inner being of the *sefirot*. The World of Emanation is the vessel for Adam Kadmon.[23] Therefore a vessel is a reality that has the quality of revelation. It mediates or transmits between one reality and another. When the thin ray of light moved into the *tehiru*, it assumed the mystical shape of Adam Kadmon. Lights issued from his head and body to form harmonious and unified higher worlds.[24] But this divine equilibrium was soon to be broken by that which emanated from his eyes. Each of the ten points of light that exited the eyes of Adam Kadmon was cloaked in its own characteristic (vessel). They generated the sefirotic worlds. The vessels that possessed *tikkun* sustained their lights and lived. The vessels without *tikkun* shattered and died.[25] Each *sefira* hypostasized independently, disconnected from the whole. They transmitted blindly from his eyes as atomized points and as a negative plurality, and therefore as nonintegrated, separate entities apart from the divine unity of this Creation. As divine emanations formed in the lower vessels, *din* was concentrated in the vessels to such an extent that the tension between it and divine lights caused them to break. "The *sefirot* separated from each another . . . because the universe was created by judgment [*din*], which is fear."[26] The emanations—or vessels—that were created to clothe, sustain and give the light specific characteristics failed. Vessels without *tikkun* shattered because they could not bear the impression caused by their lights.

Only the vessels of the three highest *sefirot* survived. The last *sefira*, *malkhut* (*Shekhinah*) survived but was damaged. This was the most profound crisis of all living phenomenon: *shebirath ha-kelim*—breaking of the vessels. Adam Kadmon's atomized points are symbols that point toward a greater meaning, of an outer world in conflict with inner worlds, moving toward a new state of being. His state of mind was without *tikkun*.[27] Inflexible, rigid and disunified lights clashed with the harmonious lights from the upper worlds.

Cataclysmic disharmony descended through the primal space. This disharmony awakened all slumbering *din*, which, in turn, activated the potentiality for evil. The resultant energy from the clash of these emanations transformed the nature of the primal space from one of unity to one with two extremes that proceeds from the highest (inner realm, Adam Kadmon) and moves progressively through all worlds to the lowest (externalized realm of matter, *klippoth*). While most energy from the clash of emanations returned to higher worlds, some dispersed into the realm of matter and is of three forms:

1. Sparks from divine light (emanations—vessels—with impressions of divine light remaining on them), *sefirot* 4–10;
2. Sparks from the inner world of Adam Kadmon;
3. *Din* (aroused *din* and disharmony generated by shattered vessels— "chards" or shapes of energy attracted to outer realms).

Every element of Creation, from the Creator to the most insignificant pre-cosmic sub-particle, bore the mark of this catastrophe. The rich deep glow of divine sparks shone through the pre-cosmic dust (all deeply and tragically intermixed) that would eventually evolve to form the slag of *klippoth* and thereby set the stage for the appearance of humankind, that would evolve from the wreckage of this sefirotic world. *"The Great Flood [was] like breaking of the vessels, as great abundance of water on the Earth . . . . like the increase of lights that fell on the Malkhut."*[28] Creation split into inner and outer realms. The tenth *sefira*, *Shekhinah*, torn apart from the undifferentiated unity in the inner world and trapped in the outer world, remains as the indwelling of each being as the exiled realm of God. All sefirotic worlds in the *tehiru* have been altered. The fabric of existence is pulled between two poles, like a conflict of ontologies between clarity and chaos. Sparks from divine light, *din* and pre-matter wrestle to evolve in the thick, swollen world of *klippoth*, while higher worlds work to rebalance them again.

In order to stay in step with Lurianic teaching, it is important to stress that Luria did not depict breaking of the vessels as the first such catastrophe of its kind to occur; he taught rather that it should be viewed as part of the process of Creation's clarification and re-harmonization in evolution so that all worlds and realities will reflect each other more brightly and more fluently in God. Successive upheavals of such magnitude are necessary and resolve themselves under the Ineffable's stabilizing and rebuilding influence. Every potentiality and the roots of evil—neglected dark corners of *en sof* that contain residue of divine sefirotic activity—will ultimately regenerate into the harmony and fullness of the Divine One. The doctrine of *tikkun* requires the restoration of the inner and outer cosmos.

Repair of Previous Worlds: The Kings of Edom

Isaac Luria's idea of breaking of the vessels and its role in the evolving process of creation originated from an event described in detail in *Idra Rabba* and *Idra Sutta* of the *Zohar*. There was, at one time, a destruction of worlds that occurred before the creation of our own cosmos. These worlds were given freedom to develop under the influences of God, but their inhabitants—*the Kings of Edom*—were possessed with excessive severity and consequently broke apart and were destroyed. Lack of harmony between male and female, love and severity, degenerates unity that sustains life and ultimately causes destruction of the world. Spiritual vestiges from previously failed worlds lay as dead in the sefirotic wreckage. They had fallen to its lowest realm and represent passive being in a place where the feminine principle of strict judgment (*din*) rules and where everything sags under the resistance and lassitude of matter. Such a place is for the rearing and uplifting of guilty souls who have come from the ruins of older worlds to bear the yoke of matter. Souls work to unite *malkhut* (feminine) with *Ze'ir Anpin* (masculine) through good deeds to uplift the sparks and thereby purify their world.[29] They are born again continually in lower levels of Creation so that they might serve divine judgment in this way. At this point in Luria's cosmogony, it is up to God to repair the destruction of his new Creation and to resurrect—regenerate—the dead kings of older worlds as part of his unfolding: The vessels ". . . *were born without tikkun, shattered and died to create external shells. External shells are necessary in the world to reward the good and righteous and to punish the wicked, who were later created . . . . And behold the contraction was Din. It destroyed so that it could repair.*"[30]

The roots of evil, residual elements of sefirotic activity and lost *sefirot* from shattered worlds (Edom) brought on by hypertrophy of *din* took full form to see the face of God: The orphaned darkness joins the unfolding of Creation so that all worlds will reflect each other more completely and radiantly within the divine will. It is as if the Godhead exercised discipline of mind to absorb its own spiritual readjustment and clarification through an ordeal, a sort of *katharsis Dei*, in order to mitigate and reintegrate negative, pre-existent elements in Itself.

In millennia hence, when creatures populate lower worlds, inner longing toward reunion and meditations toward this lost harmony will be the deepest secret of every living moment. *All phenomena and the meaning of each inner world occur according to the secret law of tikkun. Our cosmos came about from the moral imperative of a defaulted process and* ". . . *it represents a crisis in the divine life which disturbed the original harmony and diverted the intended development from its path so that it now oscillates between destruction and restoration, descent and ascent.*"[31] *And while we are the subjects of the moral imperative that sprang from this process, Isaac Luria taught that souls and cosmos originated from the realm of Lucifer (cf. glimmering klippoth) and that one is fully redeemable with or without contemplation or sefirotic reflection.*[32]

God and Repair of the First Breaking of the Vessels

To this point, Creation has evolved in the mind of God and events have been of the spirit. But now *Shekhinah* and divine lights have been trapped in the wide universe of matter, mixing and warming in questionable coexistence. The roots of other worlds—potentialities of beings that would spring from this coexistence and would live partitioned in material exile—are active. While divine inner realms lay deeply hidden, outer confused worlds drifted deeper into the clutches of matter and disorder. The rhythm of the *sefirot* seeks to reharmonize and to heal, but is now incomplete. The *tehiru* has been transformed into the world of chaos. *Sefirot* are not connected. "Male" and "female" no longer live in primal undifferentiated unity as before. Both must now enter upon a new plane and must manifest themselves under new aspects. The Divine One *seeks to mend*—to atone for rifts of the past—as Adam Kadmon strives to reintegrate all worlds and to restore the original unity that was ruined by breaking of the vessels. Adam Kadmon mended the worlds emanating a new light that would cleanse the sparks of their dross. His image reflected a deeper unity so that each *sefira* reflected a *face of God (partsuf)*[33]—a particular aspect of God's personality—to inner worlds of all Creation. While the worlds of *sefirot* still move under the pulse of *tsimtsum*, the ten *sefirot* joined together to mesh more fully with the poor state of disturbed worlds shaken by *shebirath ha-kelim*. The five Countenances are:

1. Crown or Divine Will *Arich Anpin* (the patient one), *partsuf* of *keter*, *sefira 1*;
2. Father, *Abba*, *partsuf* of *chochma*, *sefira 2*;
3. Mother, *Ima*, *partsuf* of *bina*, *sefira 3*;
4. Creating God, *Ze'ir Anpin*, (the impatient one), *partsufim* of *chessed, din, tiferet, nesach, hod, yesod, sefirot 4–9*;
5. *Indwelling* Nukva (Rahel and Leah), partsuf *of* malkhut (Shekhinah), sefira 10.

Each *partsuf* is composed of two forces: masculine (*chessed*, giving limitlessly) and feminine (*din*, limitation of masculine abundance). "*Ze'ir Anpin* and *Nukva* shine into the *kelipot* because their origins are there. . . . They shine into the *kelipot* and give it spiritual life in the secret of eleven ingredients of incense.[34]" They give vital soul, *nefesh*—libido—to the Earth. ". . . Ze'ir Anpin is the sun. His sheath is *Nukva*. She cloaks his severe judgments. . . ."[35] C. G. Jung notes: "The sun . . . reflects the visible God of this world [it is] the vital force of our own soul that we call libido and its essence is to bring forth right and wrong, good and evil. . . . The unceasing prerogative of the libido is to project itself onto the cosmos."[36] *Ze'ir Anpin* and *Nukva* are Elohim—the Upper Adam.

The *partsufim* healed the sefirotic worlds—*atsilut* (emanation), *beriah* (creation), *jezira* (forming), and *asiyah* (making). They ascended to *atsilut* thanks to the unifying power of the *partsu-fim*. But shells—*klippoth*—still lay in the way of reconciliation between outer and inner worlds.

There is a living, collective consonance that reflects fluently among the forming worlds of creation, form and angelics, under the realm of *Shekhinah*, bounded by the World of Emanation. But they live in precarious balance. It is now up to Adam to liberate the remaining sparks from the lowest realm (*klippoth*).

Adam and the Second Breaking of the Vessels

Adam was a spiritual being that lived among multi-existences in divine inner consciousness (*mohin*) of *Elohim* within the four worlds. "He was comprised of all souls that were part of the six thousand years that would form our world. His limbs we re made from these souls."[37] His task was a daunting one: In spite of the disorder and severity that so complicated the realm of matter, Adam had to free the divine sparks. But just as much as Adam Kadmon failed to sustain unity with God at the spiritual level, Adam did the same at the anthropo-morphic level. And as Adam Kadmon sought to reunify the disharmony (scattered sparks) caused by his failure through *tikkun*, Adam scattered them again in his own attempt. The totality and fervor of Adam's meditations and spiritual actions failed, and he fell, as did countless sparks and souls from higher worlds with him, broken to pieces into the material world of *klippoth*. It is in this way that Adam passed the sacred imperative of *tikkun* to mankind: "When he sinned, the souls vanished from him because shells—external forces—took control of him. The remnants of these souls shed from him and fell into the depths of matter. . . ."[38] *Just as Adam Kadmon's imperfection resulted in the first schebirath ha-Kelim, Adam's resulted in the second. "And when the souls that were in Adam fell into matter, they mingled among the four winds of the world and took his dust. Each of the seventy officers of the nations of the world is in the realm of matter and took his part [from Adam]."*[39] Mystics and alchemists of the Middle Ages confirmed these secret teachings of the kabbalah in their own visions of divine truth. *The Second Adam is there, in matter, transfigured into eternity:*

From these Latin treatises it is clear that the latent, hidden demiurg that sleeps in matter is identical with *homo philosophicus, the Second Adam*. He is the higher, spiritual humanity, the Adam Kadmon, . . . Although the First Adam was mortal . . . the Second Adam is immortal because he consists of a pure imperishable essence.[40]

The state of souls is linked inexorably with that of the fragmented disunity of Adam's:

And now behold what damage was done by his sin. Adam's body was from the world of *Yetsirah*, but only his spirit resides there now. His existence is strewn among various levels. And his body and lower soul are now in this world, the world of *Asiyah*. These things caused much spoilage among the worlds.[41]

The worlds descended and *asiyah* mixed so completely with *klippoth* that they joined. Mankind, composed of matter and spirit, evolved from this resultant new world. *The divine degeneration that proceeded from the Godhead (tsimtsum), through Adam Kadmon (shebirath ha-kelim) and Adam (second shebirath ha-kelim), now faces mankind with a real and terrifying challenge that has only one solution:*

> The intensity of Lurianic demands is most unusual. A person who accepts this world view and the ethical and religious consequences of the idea of *tikkun* must always be under enormous pressure. Every mundane or apparently unimportant deed may carry endless cosmic meaning. A spark freed by charity now may be the last and only one, and the completion of the deed may bring forth the redemption immediately. . . . Ethical demands, therefore, assume an intensity of cosmic meaning and symbolical significance never before achieved in any Jewish ethical system.[42]

Adam and the Fall of Divine Consciousness

What did the breaking apart and fall of Adam mean? While breaking of the vessels signified outer worlds in conflict with inner worlds that were moving toward a new state of being—the outer world of plurality—the breaking apart of Adam signified the new state of being that had finally arrived—*ontological consciousness*.

When Adam was created, *Ze'ir Anpin's* divine inner consciousness (*mohin*) only came from the side of Ima, located in his *keter*. . . . He was created to repair the upper worlds through good deeds. . . . And behold, while Adam was repairing *Ze'ir Anpin* and his *Nukva*, he wanted to fix *Ze'ir Anpin's keter* that was then very small. . . . Adam wanted to increase the size of his *keter*. . . . But this small size was necessary because it awaited its proper increase of size from divine inner consciousness of *Abba*. The sin of eating from the Tree of Knowledge symbolizes the grasping of external forces that entered before *Abba's* divine consciousness could enter into *Ze'ir Anpin's keter*, so that it would abrogate their grasping. [43]

All sin lay in the desire to increase the *keter* of *Ze'ir Anpin* before its time, that is, before the divine consciousness of *Abba* could enter. Because he erred, resultant disharmony among *partsufim* caused his and the *Shekhinah's* exile. Knowledge limited to the outer world ensnared the true vision that lay within Adam's grasp.[44] In exchange for knowledge and life unfolding with co-sympathy boundlessly, Adam chose limited knowledge, i.e., *ontological consciousness: "This is the great flaw—external forces grasp into the very roots of divine inner consciousness and knowledge. They cling to elements of evil. The fall of inner knowledge brought on disturbances that limited grace to flow within it so that it might balance strength and severity."*[45] Hence the duality that pervades existence up to this day: Male separated from female, above from below, good from evil, upper waters from lower waters, life from death, Tree of Life from Tree of Knowledge, etc. The vessels and Adam were divine instruments to serve Creation.

Adam was a victim caught in the divine momentum of this descending process toward which mankind is its result and ultimate redeemer. "The vessels descended twice. They first descended of themselves because they were not able to bear the great light. They were forced to descend a second time because of the sin of Adam."[46] Mankind must turn from evil, do good, and correct the deficiencies. Therefore, every sin in the outer world repeats the sin of Adam and breaking of the vessels. Its effect resounds throughout divine worlds: *"The reality of humanity's influence upon the Divine is the foundation of foundations of the kabbalah of the Ari."*[47]

Every deed of healing through *tikkun* helps to reharmonize all worlds and, ultimately, rejoins the *Shekhinah* with God. The more certain there is profound darkness, the greater the light will be that will finally overcome it.

God and Repair of the Second Breaking of the Vessels

Unity of the Godhead has been split. It must enter separately upon this new plane in order to create into the living moment of each creature. *Shekhinah* (Rahel) and her male counterpart, *Ze'ir Anpin*, once formed the face of God—*partsuf*—in unity. They now make up two realms: *partsuf* and *Shekhinah*. In this realm of existence, God moves into the inner worlds of all Creation as the active creating power in the visage of *Ze'ir Anpin*, while the *Shekhinah* receives it for all inner worlds. God's personality is a duality as well as a transcendent unity during each moment of creation. *Ze'ir Anpin* is like a human microcosm. "When *Ze'ir Anpin* ascends, he raises up with him the light that emanated toward his place. . . . He is returning and raising these sparks of holiness that have *become stagnated.*"[48]

One can not overestimate the power and fullness of meaning that the personality of God bears upon the hidden soul. Its most redeeming effect occurs when a creature joins this divine event with its own in *tikkun*. Isaac Luria sought to restore the *partsufim* and to channel their inner consciousness (*mohin*) through the power of mystical intention—*kavvanot*. "Through the practice of *kavvanot* . . . the mystic took an active role in bringing together the shattered superstructure, mending the broken vessels."[49] A creature that opens its heart with the genuine fullness of healing and meditation toward God (*tikkun*) transcends the earthly profanity of prayer and enters into *kavvanot*:

> Since *kavvanot* is of a spiritual nature, it directly affects spiritual worlds and can be an especially powerful factor if it is completed by the right [person] at the right place. The process of restitution of all things to their true place requires . . . not only an impulse which originates from God, but also an impulse which originates from the

creature's religious action. All true life and every real healing of the breach that pervades the worlds arise from the interrelationship and meeting of the divine and human impulse.[50]

Klein writes:

> Everything that is written in the Torah, every act one performs . . . is an action and principle embedded in the cosmic prehistory of the universe, is embedded in the pre-history of existence. For this reason every performance of Divine commandments and prayer (i.e., meditation with *kavanah*) affects *all existence, even pre-existence*.[51]

The Beginning and End: Tikkun

Tikkun started with *en sof* and lives, but only inconclusively, in the inner worlds of all creatures. Its grand scale and timeless momentum can never be absorbed during the snapshot of a single lifetime and the challenge that it bears upon a being's task in life extends beyond its contemporary and profane concerns and takes on full meaning only after bearing the weight of many worlds. Reincarnation (*Gilgul*) is part of the process of *tikkun* and Isaac Luria taught that each person's task is to *restore one's original spiritual form* while working through many lifetimes to suspend that disharmony in the inner worlds that occurred after breaking of the vessels and the fall of Adam.

Every soul has such a primal form within itself [that has been] affected by the mark of the world, which it must set right and purify. That restitution process is carried out in the events that the Tora condones or forbids in the soul of the human being while the human being restores the profound spiritual form of its being to its original self again through the fulfillment of the 613 commandments of the Tora, according to an old microcosmic motif of the Talmud [which states that] the 613 commandments of the Tora correspond to the 613 parts of the body.[52]

Although one might view *tikkun* as the third and final part of Isaac Luria's ideas on Creation—restitution and the eventual redemption of fallen creatures—it is actually its most universal characteristic and embodies the essence of his entire cosmogony. It has been contained in each moment of creation from the first act of *tsimtsum* onward.

Much like the movements of a complex classical drama, events cascade tragically and predictably from the divine to the spiritual and finally to the temporal realms, while the same leitmotif and inner structure play themselves out toward the transcendent meaning and redeeming power that leave the *dramatis personae* transfigured: Every subject of Creation suffers from its own innocence of becoming and must fall or break apart as it strives toward the unity that it has lost. *While each creature seeks to atone for the imperfection given to it by Creation, God seeks to atone for the Creation that caused the imperfection.* *Tikkun* reflects the ineffable meaning of an eternally changing moment of the personality of God that discloses itself to a righteous soul; to God, it is merely the way to the beginning:

> *Tikkun*—the way to the end of all things—is equally the way to [their] beginning. The teaching of the secrets of creation and of the unfolding of all things from God, becomes conversely the teaching of salvation as the return of all things to their original contact with God. Everything that mankind does acts in some way upon this very complex process of *tikkun*. All phenomenon and all worlds have an outer [face] as well as an inner face and, accordingly, Luria teaches the outer [face] of the worlds is determined by religious action and by completion of the commandments of the Torah.[53]

Preparing for Kabbalah

Translated and edited by Zechariah Goldman
Special thanks to Yrachmiel Tilles
Ascent of Safed, Ari Road & Beck Lane,
P.O. Box 296, Zefat, Israel

I the author, adjure on the great name of G-d, anyone into whose hands these [kabbalistic] pamphlets fall, that he should read this introduction. If his soul desires to enter the chamber of this wisdom, he should accept upon himself to complete and fulfill all that I write, and the former of Creation will testify upon him, that to him will not come damage to his body and soul, and to all that is his, and not to others, because of his running after good, and one who comes to purify and come close, first before everything fear of G-d, to attain fear of punishment, for awe of G-d's greatness that is the more internal fear, he will not attain, except from the maturation of wisdom.

His essential involvement in this knowledge should be to eliminate the thorns from the vineyard, for those who engage in this wisdom are therefore called tenders of the field. And certainly the evil shells will be aroused against him, to seduce him and to cause him to sin; therefore, he should be watchful that he not come to sin even unintentionally, so that they will have no relation to him. Accordingly, it is necessary to guard against [adopting] leniencies [in Torah law], for the Holy One Blessed Be He is exacting with the righteous, like a thread of hair. For this reason, he needs to abstain from meat and wine during weekdays, and he needs [to heed] the admonition of "turn from evil and do good; and pursue peace."

Pursue peace: it is necessary to seek peace, and not to be demanding in one's home, whether for an insignificant or a significant matter and certainly a person should not succumb to anger, G-d forbid!

And he needs to distance himself to the ultimate distance [from evil].

Turn from Evil

To be cautious in all the details of the commandments, and even the words of the Sages for these are included in [the negative commandment] do not stray [from the word that I [G-d] command you].

To rectify the damage [one has done] before one goes to the coming world.

To be careful not to get angry even when disciplining his children; in principle, he should not get angry at all.

In addition, he needs to be watchful of arrogance, specifically in matters pertaining [to his observance] of Halacha for the power [of arrogance] is great, and in this regard arrogance is a terrible sin.

With every pain he suffers, he should examine his deeds, and [then] return to G-d.

He should also immerse [in a *mikva*] at the necessary time [as soon as possible after any seminal emission].

He should also sanctify himself during marital relations so that he should not [egoistically/sensually] benefit.

There should not pass any night, [where he does not] think every night what he did during the day, and [he should] confess [and repent].

He should also minimize his business dealings, and if he has no livelihood, except through business, he should intend that Tuesday and Wednesday from noon and on, the intention should be [that these times are set aside] to the service of his Creator.

Any speech that is not of a *mitzva* and necessary, he should refrain from, and even in a matter of a *mitzva* he should desist [from speaking] during prayer.

And Do Good

To awaken at [Torah defined] midnight to recite the order [of the *Tikkun Chatzot*] in sackcloth and ashes, and great crying, and with intention [fulfilling], all that comes out of his mouth. And afterwards he should immerse in Torah for whatever time he can be without sleep, and at least a half hour before dawn, he should awaken to immerse in Torah study.

He should go to the synagogue before dawn, before the obligation of *talit* and *tefillin*, to be watchful that he should be one of the first of the ten [men that make a *minyan*].

Before entering [the synagogue], he should accept upon himself the positive commandment "and you shall love your neighbor as yourself," and only then enter.

To complete the hint [alluded to in the word] *tzadik* [*tzadi* = ninety; *dalet* = four; *yud* = ten; *kof* = 100] every day, that is [comprised of] ninety amen's, four *Kedushot*, ten *Kadishes*, 100 Blessings.

Not to interrupt his awareness from [the sensations of holiness and consciousness emanating from] his *tefillin* during prayer, except for Amida and while engaged in Torah study.

It is necessary to be wrapped in *talit* and *tefillin* when he immerses himself in Torah study [during the day and afternoon].

To meditate, during prayer, on the [kabbalistic] intentions, as it is written in *Etz Chaim*.

That he always places before his eyes the [Divine] Name, a product of four [letters] *Havaya(h)* [Yod- Hey-Vav-Hey] and he should veer from it, as it is written I have placed G-d before me always.

That he meditatively focus while reciting all the blessings, and specifically the blessings before enjoyment [made over eating in general].

His labor in Torah needs to be, *Pardes*, and do not think that they will reveal to him secrets of Torah when he is empty of knowledge, as it is written [in Scripture that] [G-d] gives wisdom to the wise. And one needs to be cautious that he not let escape from his mouth anything of this wisdom, that he has not heard from a man who is not worthy to depend on, as Rabbi Shimon Bar Yochai and his colleagues have warned.

Anatomy of the Creation

Special thanks to Yrachmiel Tilles
Ascent of Safed, Ari Road & Beck Lane,
P.O. Box 296, Zefat, Israel

From Likutei Torah (Chumash HaAri,
Bereishit, p. 6) in the writings of the Arizal.
Translation and commentary by Avraham Sutton
"In the beginning, G-d created the
heavens and the earth . . . " (Gen. 1:1)

In man himself, we also find Earth and Heaven. The diaphragm
[right below the solar plexus] divides the organs of breathing
[the respiratory system] from the organs of digestion. In the
larger universe, this [diaphragm] corresponds to the firmament
[atmosphere] that is spread out over the Earth.

The diaphragm is thus seen as separating between the more spiritual aspects of the body [Heaven] and the lower, more physical aspects [Earth].

Above it [the diaphragm] we thus have the heart, the lungs, the brain, etc., while below, we have the more corporeal and gross physical [organs]. According to this, the upper half of a person is the "heavenly" half, and the lower half is the "earthly" half. Man, in this sense, is a miniature world.

We see this in the verse, "Let us make Man in our image and in our likeness" (Gen. 1:26), wherein the G-dly *Tzelem* ["image"] refers to soul of man. The soul, in other words, is what the Torah calls [the real] man [Adam]. This is seen in another verse that states, "Do not anoint the flesh of a man . . . " (Num. 30:32). The Torah indicates clearly that the "clothes" are not the man.

At the beginning of *Shaarei Kedusha*, Rabbi Chaim Vital similarly writes:

> It is known to the masters of the sciences that a person's body is not his essence [but rather a vehicle for his soul]. The body is therefore referred to as "Man's flesh," as in the verse, "Cover me [my essence] with skin and flesh, and surround me with bones and sinews." (Job 10:11) It is also written, "Do not anoint the flesh of a man . . ." (Num. 30:32).

The inner being is the true self, while the body is merely a garment.

[In both these verses] we find that the inner being is the true self, while the body is merely a garment with which the soul covers itself while [sojourning] in this world. At the moment of death, when the soul departs, this garment is removed, and it is clothed in a pure, clean, spiritual garment. It is thus written, "Remove the soiled garments . . . and you shall be clothed in fine robes"; (Zach. 3:4) these "fine robes" are none other than the "rabbinical mantle" [in Aramaic, *chaluka d'rabbanan*, or spiritual energy body with which the soul is clothed when it enters the Garden of Eden].

Just as a tailor makes a suit of clothes to fit a person's physique, so did the Holy One Blessed Be He make the body as a garment to clothe the soul. And just as a suit is cut and tailored according to the exact proportions of a person's limbs, so did the Holy One make the body according to the pattern of the soul. The body thus has 248 organs/limbs, along with 365 blood vessels that connect them and transport life-giving blood from one to the other, similar to a system of pipes.

With regard to the body, the verse states, "Let us *make* . . ." [indicating the level of *asiyah*]. For, indeed, the body is made from materials provided by the physical world. The same is [partially] true of angels. When they descend to our lower world, they too must "dress up" in a body that conforms to the laws of this material plane.

Concerning the ability of angels to "dress up" in a physical form, the Zohar states: "It has been established: These [angels are able to exist in this world because they] appear to humans in human form. And if you should ask: How do they transform themselves thus? They transform through many colors [energy frequencies]. When they are ready to actually descend, they dress up in [take on the molecular structure of] the Earth's atmosphere, and they appear as humans." (Zohar I:58a)

In another place, the Zohar makes an important connection between the way angels descend into our world and the way that we (our souls) ascend into the spiritual dimension: "[At the moment of death] the spirit [ruah] separates [and divests itself] of the lower soul [nefesh in order to [rise up and] enter the lowest level of the Garden of Eden [the world of yetzirah There it 'clothes' itself in the atmosphere of that Garden, in exactly the opposite manner that the supernal angels 'clothe' themselves in physicality when they descend to this world." (Zohar I:81a)

These angels are of the level of ruah [the world of yetzirah] about whom it is written, "He makes His Messenger-Angels Spirits" (Ps. 104:4). This means that He makes the Messenger-Angels of yetzirah descend to the world of asiyah—Action [the physical world] as messengers. The ruah-Spirit of Man, on the other hand, goes up from the physical world to the lowest level of the Garden of Eden and "wears" the garb of that dimension. She [the soul] is refined there and has tremendous pleasure, . . .

This is why the three angels who visited Abraham appeared to eat.

The Zohar (I:102a), Talmud (Bava Metzia 86b), and Midrash (Bereishit Rabba 48:14; Shemot Rabba 47:5) all cite the famous teaching that, "One should never deviate from the customs of the place he visits" (the Jewish equivalent of: "When in Rome do as the Romans"). Concerning Moses, it is written, "He remained there with G-d [on the mountain] for forty days and forty nights without eating bread or drinking water" (Ex. 34:28), and "I remained on the mountain forty days and forty nights, without eating food or drinking water." (Deut. 9:9) The Midrash asks: Is it possible for a human being to go without food and drink for so long [and not die]? Rather, Moshe went up to Heaven where there is no food, so he did not eat. [The Midrash adds at the end of 47:5: So how did he survive if he didn't eat? He was nourished by the radiance of the Divine Presence. And do not be surprised. For the Angels above that carry the Divine Throne are similarly nourished from the radiance of the Divine Presence.] Conversely, when the angels descended to Abraham, they seemed to eat and drink, as it is written, "He stood over them and they ate under the tree" (Gen. 18:8). The Midrash and Zohar both exclaim: Do you think that those supernal beings really ate? It only seemed that they were eating! Since angels are fire, the food was consumed as they put it in their mouths. All the while it seemed that they were eating like normal humans.

The same is true of the soul of man. [In order to be born] it must dress up in the atmosphere of this world.

This explains, as well, why the verse is spoken in the plural, "Let *us* make . . . ." The soul is from the Blessed One. [In order to be born] it descends and dresses up in the atmosphere of the worlds [or actually dresses "down" in and through the various atmospheres of each lower world/dimension, each of which contributes another garment which the soul dons as it approaches our gross physical plane of existence].

[Speaking to these various levels and their angelic inhabitants, G-d] thus says, "Let *us* make a garment for man, i.e., the soul, with which he will be able to descend into the dimension of *asiyah.*" Man will then be "in our image" [in Hebrew, *be'tzalmenu,* from the word *Tzelem,* referring to the spiritual image of the angels, and "in our likeness" [in Hebrew, *ki'demutenu*], referring to the physical garments within which they [the angels] clothe themselves when they enter the atmosphere of this world.

We thus see that man consists of two aspects: *Adam Elyon,* Superior Man—the soul—and *Adam Tachton,* Inferior Man—the body.

The Ten Sephirot

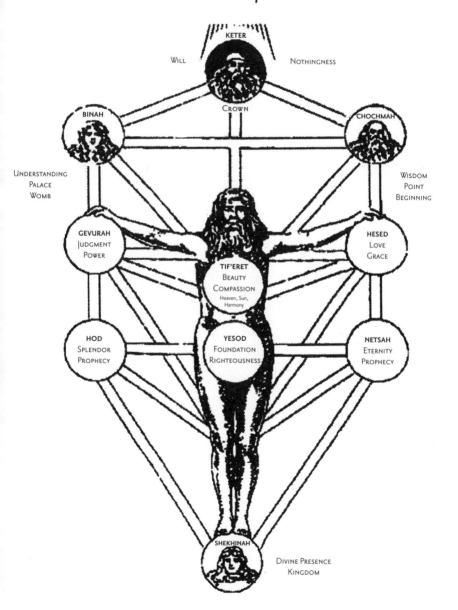

KETER

WILL   NOTHINGNESS

CROWN

BINAH

CHOCHMAH

UNDERSTANDING
PALACE
WOMB

WISDOM
POINT
BEGINNING

GEVURAH
JUDGMENT
POWER

HESED
LOVE
GRACE

TIF'ERET
BEAUTY
COMPASSION
Heaven, Sun,
Harmony

HOD
SPLENDOR
PROPHECY

YESOD
FOUNDATION
RIGHTEOUSNESS

NETSAH
ETERNITY
PROPHECY

SHEKHINAH

DIVINE PRESENCE
KINGDOM

The Sacred Name: The Tetragrammaton

The four-letter Ineffable Name of God (YHVH), signifying the eternal and transcendent revelation of God.

The Sacred Faces

Arikh Anpin: Wills existence through all worlds.
The Patient One, large face.

Abba: God the Father; intuitive insight; fully
articulated form.

Ima: God the Mother; intellectual powers;
emotions; Creation.

Ze'ir Anpin: Light of grace. Individual leadership of
divine attributes. Coexists with, yet is
independent of that which is part of him
self—the *Nukva*. The Impatient One, the
small face. Male counterpart of *Nukva*.

Nukva: True and direct root of created beings.
Not connected in existence, yet indivisible

in life and spiritual growth with *Ze'ir Anpin*. Female counterpart of *Ze'ir Anpin*. Develops from the *sefira malkhut*, the kingdom, the active divine presence within.

Indwelling Worlds

Adam Kadmon: Infinite and purest light of Creation.

Atsilut: Deepest immanent world that is closest to the Infinite Light. World within, as a storm of unformed primordial matter, below *atsilut*.

Beriah: The spiritual abode of *seraphim*.

Jezira: Immanent world whose primordial matter receives form; the spiritual abode of living beings mentioned in Ezekiel's vision of the Merkava.

Asiyah: Immanent world of matter, receiving "form" from the higher world of *jezira*. It is limited by its spiritual and physical dimensions as we see them now in our own cosmos.

Levels of the Soul

Yechidah: Soul's one-ness with ultimate level of consciousness in the Divine One.

Chayyah: Soul's life force within moral consciousness.

Neshamah: Soul's intellect within sustained existence.

Ruah: Soul's breath within the heart of love and emotions.

Nefesh: Soul's blood within the body in this world of living beings.

Prayer

Before the study of the Ari, Rabbi Isaac Luria.
May his merit, protect us. Amen.

Master of the Universe, Lord of Lords, Father of mercy and
forgiveness, we bow before you, God, our God, and God of our
fathers, You who have brought us near to Your law and to the
worship of Your divine service and have given to us a share in
the secrets of Your holy law and worship of Your divine service.
What are we and what are our lives worth that you give us such
a great grace as this? Because of Your mysteries, we lay down
our supplications before you so that you might forgive all of
our sins and transgressions. And do not let our sins separate us
from You. And may it be your will, God, our God and God of
our fathers that you prepare our hearts to fear and to love You.
And may your ears listen to these our words and may You open
our hearts so that they are not denied the secrets of Your law.
And may our studies be pleasant before the Seat of Your honor

like the savory smell of a sacrifice. And may You emanate the light of the source of our souls over us during all of our examinations. And let gleam the sacred sparks of holiness among your blessed servants who receive these Your words in the universe. Bestow upon us the goodness and the merit of their fathers, their learning, innocence and holiness, so that we do not stumble among these holy words. And in their goodness let our eyes be enlightened in what we study, as is written in the words of the kind Psalmist of Israel "Open Thou mine eyes, that I may behold." (Ps. 119:18) This is because God will give wisdom, knowledge and understanding from His mouth. "Let what I say and what I think be pleasing before You, God, my Rock and my Redeemer."†

†*Ets hayim*, Vol. 2. The volume begins with Gate 25, *Derushe ha-teslem*. That page is not numbered but the next page is *Dalet* =4. The first page is [p. 3]. The prayer is opposite it on [p. 2].

The Kings of Edom

1   Divine inner consciousness was drawn to *Abba* and *Ima* from the crown (*keter*).

2   Divine emanations from *Abba* and *Ima* joined in unity and the seven kings were born.

3   The kings reigned in the land of Edom before any king reigned over the children of Israel.

4   The secret of everything from the Earth lies within the mystery of the kings of the land of Edom.

5   The kings are called points. A point is the kingdom, *malkhut*.

6   The kingdom was born in the secret of the feminine, which encircles the masculine.

7   The kings were born from what is circular, which is the soul.

8   But they were not united, nor inside of each other, nor together in lines. In the beginning there was no *tikkun*. The image of these ten points was the same, as if each point had one lone face. Some were in the image of separate people, each facing his or her own way, without love between them. Their vessels, therefore, died because they could not endure the light alone and disunited. . . . When the points left Adam Kadmon as he contracted himself, a rift opened, causing a split in his navel. These events relate closely to the death of the kings.

9   Oneness (*tikkun*) is achieved by way of lines.

10   Before *tikkun* was achieved, each king was on the back of the other.

11   Whenever one point is on the back of the other point, each is separated from the other and forms the public domain.

12   Mercy is the right line, severity the left line, and compassion the middle line.

13   The first three kings were born with mercy and unity.

14 The seven lower kings were born without *tikkun*, one beneath the other.

15 The Idra Rabba says: "How long must we sit, limited within our own self?"

16 The first three Kings of Edom did not lack *tikkun* and did not die.

17 The remaining seven kings died because they were born with no *tikkun* at all.

18 Connection causes existence and coming into being. They say that if one takes ten reeds, each of them may be broken if they are not united. But if one takes only three together, they will exist and not be broken.

19 Before the unity (*tikkun*), there was no love in the ten *sefirot*, only fear among them.

20 The *sefira malkhut* is a clouded window that does not shine, exiled from its self.

21 The *sefirot* separated from each another . . . because the universe was created by judgment, which is fear.

22 The universe could not continue to exist because the kings perished. God participated in the universe by giving it mercy. It is *tikkun*.

23   The lower six points that would form *Ze'ir Anpin* exited as the images of the Kings of Edom. . . . Among these points is the *Nukva*, which is called the Earth of Edom. The points were born separated, not in the fashion of lines, each on the back of the other. They are the public domain because there was nothing unique or united in them

24   After love and uniqueness were given to the *sefirot*, the six points joined into one image.

25   *Tikkun* is of the World of Emanation. It occurred when six separate points conjoined into three lines, one with the other in unity—the private domain.

26   This is existence of one base.

27   The seven kings are the sparks that spewed forth as from a craftsman, who pounded with iron tools and brought out sparks with each stroke.

28   Severity and judgments of the powerful descended and made matter and it is Satan.

29   The kings were broken. Lights from within them departed.

30   Their shattered vessels remained behind.

31   Only the impression of 288 sparks remained in the vessels.

32 The seven kings made the powers of matter and shells (*kelipot*).

33 The death of the kings, breaking of the vessels and the fall caused the *kelipot*.

34 This was done so that there would be choice and free will.

35 External shells are needed to reward the righteous and to punish the wicked in the world, which was to be soon created.

36 The 288 sparks of the kings . . . is found in hidden secrets of the Mishna . . . the deep treacherous mountains . . . that deal in the thickness of matter, in *kelipot*, just as the mountains and hills in the secret of strong wind that breaks mountains and rocks, breaks males and females, where the snake crouches. . . . The way of the eagle of the air. . . . The way of the serpent upon the rock. . . . The way of a ship in the midst of the sea. The deceitful, strong, deep mountains are the *kelipah*.

37 When judgments unite, they increase endlessly. It is therefore necessary that they do not arise and join forces. . . . Judgment is endless fire, flame and sparks.

38 The kings are the Hebrew letters and the vessels.

39   The Flood is the image of the breaking of the vessels, the abundance of water on the Earth, like the abundance of the lights that fell on the kings.

40   There was *tikkun* for the first three kings. They were not broken. When the seven lower kings were in the womb of the mother, they existed in the image of female waters, which stirs the upper union of emanations. When the seven lower kings exited from the mother, they were the seven kings who ruled in the land of Edom. They wanted shelter in their vessels. The vessels could not tolerate this. They broke and died.

41   The secret says: "Now the earth was unformed and void" (Gen. 1:2). Since the Earth is the very last *Hey* [of the Tetragrammaton], it is therefore in the aspect of the eye. . . . It is unformed and void and this is regarding the death of the kings until their *tikkun* comes.

42   And God said: "Let there be light." And there was light.

43   The seven kings drew their light from the body of Adam Kadmon.

44   O my God, incline your ear, and hear. Open your eyes. And behold our desolations and the city upon which your name is called. For we do not present our supplication before you because of our righteousness but because

of your great compassions. . . . See our desolation. There was great desolation and the death of the kings.

45 The secret of death . . . is that one is separated and uprooted from one's own world, gone to another world below. It is like the death of the seven kings, who ruled in the land of Edom and fell below into the World of Creation. This is called death.

46 Humanity needs the blessings from the upper ones so for strength. The upper ones need help from the lower ones. . . . The upper worlds descend and live within lower levels to help and to purify the seven kings.

47 The images of the seven kings form Adam from his head to his feet that sink into the *kelipot*. And when sparks are purified and ascend, then all of mankind will be purified and the Messiah will come.

48 In order to have free will, desire, reward and punishment in the world, God created the kings and let them die.

49 The ten martyrs are the ten drops that were thrown from the nails of Joseph. . . . These ten drops clothe their souls. These clothes—not their souls—are called the bodies of the ten martyrs and are the garments of the Rabbis. This world forms the remnants that were not purified from the kings and they are the secret of the 320 sparks that were thrown from the Upper Thought. They are good and evil. The Tree of Knowledge is the remnants that were not purified from the kings, who are . . . the sparks, which were thrown from the Upper Thought.

50 The kings died because neither male nor female had been created. They were drawn from above, from divine consciousness, the Upper Thought, without the feminine, the *Nukva*. This was all before the *tikkun*, before *Atika Kadish* received *tikkun* and evolved into male and female. The kings are drops of nocturnal emission, called sparks.

51 Understand this marvelous secret. The higher souls of the ten martyrs were clothed in the garment of the Rabbis and this garment is their inner body, made from nocturnal emission.

52 They are the secret of the Tree of Knowledge, good and evil. Their souls are for holiness. They are like the lights of the vessels of the kings. Their bodies, however, are the robes of the Rabbis. They are from *Sitra Ahara*, of the Tree of Knowledge, like the vessels of the kings.

53 The vessels broke and descended to the place of death, in the secret of the Tree of Knowledge. Then the bodies that were from these vessels were fated to die so that they might be purified of the drosses that were in them. The drosses that had been in these bodies were purified by death and they became good. They then ascended,

returning to the Upper Thought again, to that place from which they had previously fallen, to the place where the vessels of the kings had also ascended in the secret of female waters so that they might be purified among the *partsufim* in *atsilut*.

54 Their souls were completely righteous—good and not evil. *Sitra Ahara* did not rule in these souls. . . . But their bodies were formed from the Tree of Knowledge and the *Sitra Ahara* therefore ruled in these bodies. She comes from rust and waste that is on the back of the gold. . . . They thus ascended and were purified in the aspects of male and female waters, as is known, until *Abba* and *Ima* join to form life [again]. . . .

55 The worlds of *atsilut*, *beriah*, *yetsirah*, and *asiyah* became pure through the purification of the kings. The most superior is *atsilut*. The worst of the dross from *atsilut* is in *beriah*. *Beriah* was made from it. And, in this manner, *yetsirah* was formed. And so also *asiyah* was formed from the dross. And in this way *asiyah* was formed. The worst that was not able to be purified remained within the secret of *kelipah*. They are very harsh judgments, unable to be purified of their drosses. And still there remained sparks of holiness behind, inside the *kelipot*. These are the eleven ingredients of incense.

56 And likewise in *atsilut*, *Atik* benefited from the most select purification; then *Arikh Anpin* benefited lesser and

such benefit of this purification continued with gradual diminishment in each *sefira* contained in each *partsuf* to the last detail.

57 The purified sparks ascend from the place to which they had fallen and enter the womb of *Nukva*. They tarry and are sweetened there during this time of conception and become like a *partsuf*.

58 The kings ruled before the children of Israel and before the *tikkun* that they must inherit.

59 The children of Israel are called kings because they are the children of kings, from the kingdom of Adam Kadmon and they shall be so until the glory of the King of Life. This king is the foundation of Adam Kadmon, the drop of whiteness.

60 *Ze'ir Anpin* and *Nukva* are the last two letters of the Tetragrammaton (*Yod Hey Vav Hey, YHVH*).

61 They are separate from *Abba* and *Ima*, who are the first two letters, *Yod Hey*.

62 And behold, in the time of exile . . . there is no complete name (Tetragrammaton), since *Ze'ir Anpin* and *Nukva* are only the last two letters, *Vav Hey*.

63 *Ze'ir Anpin* and *Nukva* descend below.

64   *Ze'ir Anpin* and *Nukva* shine into the *kelipot* because their origins are there.

65   They shine into the *kelipot* and give it life in the secret of the eleven ingredients of the frankincense. These ingredients are the life of the *kelipot*.

66   They are the life of the *kelipot* and its breath of life is drawn from the two letters *Vav* and *Hey* of the Tetragrammaton.

67   *Ze'ir Anpin* and *Nukva* ascend to the world of *atsilut* and join with *Abba* and *Ima* (*Yod* and *Hey* of the Tetragrammaton). The eleven ingredients of the frankincense, the life of the *kelipot*, flow from *Vav* and *Hey* and ascend to them as well. It is in this way that the *kelipot* is vanquished.

68   Then the Upper Name, the Tetragrammaton, is made complete.

69   The secret of death . . . means the alienation of a thing and its uprootedness from its own world, it is without direction, without guidance, as worlds beacon from below. It is like the death of the seven kings who ruled in the land of Edom and fell into Creation.

70   The kingdom is really the seven kings.

71 Whoever goes from world to world and is separated from his world wanders in death.

72 The seven kings died. Their vessels descended to the World of Creation. The kings are now *Ze'ir Anpin* and *Nukva*. *Abba* and *Ima* suffered but did not die. Their sacred powers that extend to the worlds were broken. They descended below to the world of *atsilut*.

73 There was spoilage for the sake of fixing and destruction for the sake of rebuilding.

74 It is forbidden to expand upon these things and to utter them. A discerning person will understand.

75 The image of female waters is about the holy souls. These souls are within the Kings of Edom. They must be purified so that they will ascend in the female waters. Then, male waters will join with them. Male and female waters join in the language of knowing and within these images higher souls are formed and created.

76 *Ze'ir Anpin* and *Nukva* form the divine face of Adam in righteousness.

77 The principle of circles was also established for them, because they are the image of the spirit, which establishes the soul.

78 In the time of divine conception, i.e., the *tikkun*, the kings were clarified and purified in the secret of birth (reincarnation) inside of the circles of *Abba* and *Ima*.

79 Circles were created that did not break a second time.

80 In the cells of the spleen is blackness, existence without legs. These cells are as the purifications of the kings, as the measure of one [who is lame, stump-legged and who goes forth into the world]—this is the secret of the snake whose legs were cut off: "Upon your belly shall you go." (Gen. 3:14)

81 In turning the snake on its back, one envisions the secret of the flaming sword that turns every which way, like a body that has been torn to pieces.

82 One discusses deceitful, strong, deep mountains. They are *kelipah*.

83 They are the slag of the gold like the waste of judgments.

84 There in the *kelipot*, there is *the darkness* without legs. It is glimmering matter.

85 The depths of the sea are the remnants of the purifications of the drosses of the kings.

86   The remnants of the kings are a land of drought and the shadow of death: Male and Female.

87   The seven are kingdom in the kingdom. They did not exit.

88   In the time of *tikkun*, the eighth king, Hadar, was born under the image of *Ze'ir Anpin*.

89   He is the foundation and mightier than the seven kings. They are the image of the kingdom in *Ze'ir Anpin* and *Nukva*.

90   His feminine element Metbal was born, under the image of *Nukva*.

91   They were born for the *tikkun* of Adam.

92   Hadar and Metbal entered in conception inside of *Abba* and *Ima* in righteousness. Their *Ze'ir Anpin* and *Nukva* were born in the image of higher soul so that it could establish their soul's life force in the principle of circles.

93   The seven kings died. Then the second seven points of Hadar made the secret of the two Sabbaths: masculine and feminine.

94   Hadar is of the Tetragammaton. It is spirit and righteousness. It is masculine and feminine in the kingdom from which he was born.

95 The image of the seven kingdoms is in the six *sefirot* that make *Ze'ir Anpin*.

96 They are the Tetragrammaton and the Tetragrammaton of the general Tetragrammaton that is also the name Tetragrammaton.

97 The general Tetragrammaton is the soul and it is the seven kingdoms that are in *Ze'ir Anpin* and *Nukva* and they are the seven Primeval Kings.

98 They were born from the circular.

99 Elohim is the secret of gleaming . . . it stretches from *Ze'ir Anpin* in the World of Creation until the end of the *Shekhinah*. They are the 120 combinations of Elohim. . . . They are the exterior vessels. . . . Outside of them is Elohim of Gleaming. And strange gods begin there. This is the secret of 288 sparks, which were to be purified in the realm of gleaming shells.

100 The realm of gleaming shells, on the farthest reach of *atsilut*, is holy Elohim, the Throne of Sparks. From *Ze'ir Anpin* in the World of Creation and below lie good and evil.

101 In the beginning the Upper Emanator created the Kings of Edom in the aspect of holiness that reflected judgment and severity. They were made from dregs and shells. The

Upper Emanator created them thus and in full intention so that there would be reward and punishment in the world. He took their lives so that their holy sparks would be purified. These sparks could then ascend above the shells in which they had been inextricably trapped. The shells would then remain below, far below in the secret of the drosses of gold and dregs of wine.

102 The seven lower kings had complete death within them, just as any person who might depart from this world, whose soul's sacred breath returns to God, who gave it. The body no longer has strength to grasp onto breath and soul; it loses its hold upon them, dies and returns to the dry Earth below. This is also the case with the kings whose vessels were not able to contain the great light. They died and descended to the dry Earth, the World of Creation. The souls, their sacred breath, ascended to God, to upper *Ima*, the Upper Mother. It is upper *Ima* who gives sacred lights and essence within them and who receives it when they have departed. It is therefore called death. Because everyone who descends from greatness, is separated from the world of their birth, and falls from higher ranks to lower levels is called death, as is written in *Zohar Parashat Naso Idra*. One should not say that the seven lower kings died, but rather, they descended as one who descends from his or her rank, etc. as is written: "And the King of Egypt died." See there. The defect that

occurred to the three higher kings fell and was preserved in *atsilut* itself. The only difference is that it resided in a lower place and therefore this will not be called death, just abrogation.

103 The secret of Adam Kadmon, the husband of Lilith, is: he ate, was enticed and died as is written in *Parshat Terumah* 144. The good that exists in the glowing of shells is Adam Kadmon. . . . And when he was mixed among evil, the exterior shells, he became evil. His death lies in the secret of the death of the Kings of Edom. The vessels were made from their remnants and they are the glowing that shines in them. This is therefore the Tree of Death, as mentioned in the *Tikkunim* 60.

104 And these are the glowing shells, the hide of the serpent, the outer shells that comprise all such worlds. They are of the value of the snake and are mixed with holiness. The shells of storm (stormy wind, Ez. 1:4) are the inner life of the snake. The snake has an inner world. . . . Stormy wind begins below and strives to ascend. . . . Glowing is the highest and lives within all of them. It is close to holiness. It is called the hide of the snake in the *Tikkunim*.[36]

105 Behold this is in truth the sin of Adam in the Tree of Knowledge and good and evil. His garments come from electrum. He inherited them from glowing shells. . . . It

was dressed in glowing shells, which is good and evil, called the hide of the snake.

106 After the sin of Adam, all of his garments and limbs were lost, including those that would make of the Sons of Adam of Israel of this World. They fell into gleaming shells (*Kelipah Nogah*). After having been purified, they returned, mixed among good and evil. And then, gleaming shells took the form of mankind. Mankind had power over others to cause pain and to destroy, as is mentioned in *Saba of Mishpatim*. And all of the garments of Adam fell and mixed with the evil of the shells of matter. Adam's garments form each body that lives in this world. Each body is good and evil. These garments (bodies) must be purified again by means of the commandments.

107 Adam saw that the snake was mating with Havah and he desired to do that act. Adam was created during daylight on Friday, the eve of the Sabbath. If he would have waited to mate until Friday evening . . . the mating would have been proper and all of Adam's semen would have been without evil. But since Adam chose to mate during the day, filth mixed with his semen. This signifies the Tree of Knowledge, good and evil. The snake put its filth into the daylight hours through Friday until sunset because the shells gather during this time. The shells want to receive the same holy illumination so that they

might have life during the forthcoming week. This is why it is written that one must wash the hands and the feet on the eve of the Sabbath.

108 The first three kings suffered a change. . . . But it was not really death. The seven lower kings really died.

109 I heard once from my teacher, of blessed memory, that the seven kings died because they lost their branches when they were unable to tolerate the light. But their roots remained within. And when the Upper Emanator returned to fix them, he gave the branches back to their roots and in this way they were repaired. The three upper kings in Ze'ir Anpin are the roots of the seven lower kings. When the seven lower kings lacked divine inner consciousness, they died. When they were repaired, he brought them back again to their roots in the secret of the fetus and their roots are the three upper kings. And all of the kings entered the worlds together [again] and they began their existence.

110 Oh hear the secret: "Who has measured the waters in the hollow of the hand? And meted out heaven with the span? And comprehended the dust of the Earth in a measure? And weighed the mountains in scales? And put the hills in a balance?" (Is. 40:12) It is the vessel of the living divine presence, the dust of the dry Earth. This

vessel and this dust are the kings that reigned in the land of Edom, before any king reigned over the Children of Israel. This is the secret: "And comprehended the dust of the Earth," which is the vessel of the divine living presence. It is called dust of the Earth. The Emanator spanned it from the crown through the foundation.

Divine Rebirth

1   In the beginning there was simple light called *en sof*.

2   Neither void nor did emptiness exist. All was the light of *en sof*.

3   And behold this enigma is very deep. It almost endangers the person who examines it carefully. . . . The upper light diffuses eternally. This light that radiates eternally is called *en sof*. It cannot be grasped in thought nor principle. It is abstracted and separated from all thought and it existed before all that was ever emanated or created.

4   And then he chose through his divine will to emanate and to create.

5   He did this for compassion and mercy, because if there were no one among the worlds who might receive mercy

from him, how would he be called compassionate and merciful?

6   Behold, he contracted himself in the middle of his light, in his very midpoint, leaving a void within.

7   The contraction reveals the root of justice, so that divine justice would exist in the worlds.

8   After the contraction, there remained an empty space and open void, poised in the midst of *en sof*, so that emanated and created beings could be there.

9   Behold, Adam was created by the contraction. Substance and vessels were there.

10 The contraction causes the birth of vessels. . . . But they are not truly vessels yet, except for the value of light that is in them. . . . It is perfectly pure, clear and transparently bright.

11 *En sof* contracted itself to form Adam Kadmon. Adam Kadmon was made in order to produce the points. This is emanation. These events relate closely to the abrogation of the Kings of Edom.

12 Behold, Adam Kadmon moved from the upper to the lower end of the void of emanation.

13 This void formed a circle, equidistant from all sides of its midpoint . . . such that the light of *en sof* encompassed it equally.

14 An empty space existed between the light inside the void and the light of *en sof* that surrounded it. If the case were otherwise, everything would return to how it was.

15 *En sof* surrounds the emanations within the void completely and is attached. At the summit of the upper emanation is the head and it continues to spread to the end of emanation. There is thus a beginning and an end in emanation.

16 A line of light entered into the void from the light of *en sof*. It moved from above to below.

17 The topmost point of the light is fully connected to *en sof*; the lowermost point is not.

18 And by way of this line there continues and spreads the light of *en sof* beneath.

19 And in that empty space, he emanated, created and made the entirety of all the worlds.

20 And this thin line spreads and moves from the seas of the upper light of *en sof*, to the worlds, which are in the place of higher realms in that void.

21　In the beginning, the line of light spread, extended itself and became a circle, detached from the light of *en sof*, as *en sof* surrounded the void from all sides.

22　If the circle were attached to *en sof*, it would return to the fullness that created it and dissolve in the light of *en sof* and all would return to what it was in the beginning.

23　The circle is near to the *en sof* that surrounds it without being attached to it.

24　The principle of connection and attachment of the emanated circle to *en sof* is by way of the line that traverses it, as it descends and draws light from *en sof* and emanates it, forming the circle.

25　*En sof* illuminates into beings by way of this line only. *En sof* causes the emanations that flow only into the line of light, because if *en sof* were to flood into the void from all sides, the Emanator would become the emanated, without boundary and without end.

26　The thin line is small so that the light will be drawn to the emanated in a fixed manner and end. This forms the basis of that which is emanated.

27　In the beginning, ten points exited from [Adam Kadmon] without *tikkun*.

28 They exited in the aspect of lights and vessels without *tikkun* and therefore they could not tolerate the light. *Tikkun* existed for the vessels so that they could tolerate the light.

But the vessels could still not bear the lights that formed their essence within. They broke and died.

29 They were born without *tikkun*, shattered and died for the purpose of creating external shells. External shells are necessary in the world to reward the good and righteous and to punish the wicked. They were created later.

30 After they shattered, He returned to repair them.

31 He returned to repair the vessels and to raise the holiness that was in them through *tikkun*.

32 There are ten qualities and ten *sefirot*. This means that they have number, quality and an end.

33 Behold, the line forms the first circle and it is most attached to *en sof*. It is called *keter* of Adam Kadmon.

34 Subsequently, the line moves fluidly and continuously and forms another circle inside the first circle, called *chochma* of Adam Kadmon.

35   It then continues, descending lower, and forms a third circle inside the second circle, called *bina* of Adam Kadmon.

36   And thus it continues, until the tenth circle, called *malkhut* of Adam Kadmon.

37   The line moves in a straight manner, from above to below, from the apex of the upper circle, to the nadir of the lowest, from top to bottom of all of the *sefirot*, in the secret of the straight image of mankind, that has erect height and 248 limbs. They are drawn in the image of man in three lines: right, left, middle, all of which comprise the generality of the ten *sefirot*. Each *sefira* has infinite configuration in the manner of circles.

38   Subsequently, ten more *sefirot* form *Atik Yomen*, and ten other ones, each inside of the other, form *Arikh Anpin*, and then *Abba* and *Ima*, etc., thereby completing all of emanation to the last detail. . . . There is internal light and surrounding light. Everything is in the aspect of circles.

39   In the middle of all emanation is a circle that forms in the aspect of a straight line of light. It is in the image of a circle, except that it is straight. In this circle are the aspects of *Arich Anpin, Abba, Ima, Ze'ir Anpin* and *Nukva*, and all are straight, as the Torah says, because man is in the image of God.

40   Within all circles and through their length Adam was drawn in a straight fashion.

41   This line gives light and abundance to each world.

42   It is the image of the straight light that is expressed in the form of three lines, the Upper Adam.

43   It is the aspect of straightness and not of circles.

44   There are many types of worlds that were emanated, created, formed, made and completed—thousands upon thousands and ten thousands upon ten thousands. And all of them, as if they are one, are inside that void. There is nothing outside of it.

45   And behold each and every world has ten *sefirot*. Each *sefira* is unique in each and every world. All *sefirot* are in the form of circles, each inside of the other in succession, continuing infinitely. They are like the layers of onions, one contained in the other, as concentric circles.

46   And behold, the aspect that joins all of the circles together is the thin line, that spreads from *en sof*, and moves in a continuous manner from circle to circle until the finality of their purpose.

47   It is stated in all the books of kabbalah that the worldof *atsilut* is made from the image of the ten points that exited

the eyes of Adam Kadmon. At first, these ten points exited without *tikkun*. Afterward they were repaired.

48 The first point, *keter*, possessed *tikkun*. *Arikh Anpin* is below *keter* and is part of it.

49 From the second and third points, *chochma* and *bina*, were created two faces, called *Abba* and *Ima*. *Chessed, gevurah* and *tiferet* of *Arikh Anpin* are concealed in them.

50 Subsequently, from the six points—4th, 5th, 6th, 7th, 8th, 9th—*chessed, gevurah, tiferet, nesach, hod, yesod* were made one face called *Ze'ir Anpin*.

51 And afterwards, from the tenth point, *malkhut*, there was made another face, called *Nukva* of *Ze'ir Anpin*.

52 *Nesach, hod* and *yesod* of *Arikh Anpin* are concealed in *Ze'ir Anpin* and *Nukva*.

53 Each *partsuf* is concealed each within the other, successively, until there is only one *Arikh Anpin*, which is the *keter* that includes all emanation from above to below.

54 Therefore, after the *tikkun*, the ten points formed the image of five faces: *Arikh Anpin, Abba, Ima, Ze'ir Anpin* and *Nukva*. *Atik Yomen* was concealed within *Arikh Anpin*.

55 These faces now form the image of five countenances, formed from *tikkun*, each succeeding the other in greatness.

56 *Ze'ir Anpin* is deficient compared to the higher three faces.

57 *Nukva* of *Ze'ir Anpin* was made from the fourth face, from *Ze'ir Anpin*.

58 It cannot be said that the *Nukva* of *Ze'ir Anpin* was created of ten points in the same manner as the first three faces, because, if this were so, then *Nukva's* ascent would be greater than that of *Ze'ir Anpin*. The *Nukva* is an individual point comprised of ten points of the *keter* that is in it.

59 This was not so in the beginning. Each had been separate and distinct. Each comprised an individual point, forming ten.

60 God created the worlds so that he would be complete in all his works, deeds, strengths, names of greatness, degree and honor.

61 If he does not bring his deeds and strengths to fruition, he would not be complete in them.

62 The great name, the Tetragrammaton, arises from his eternal beginning and eternal existence forever.

63   He was and is. He will be before the Creation. He will be before the existence of the Creation. He will be after these things return to what they were.

64   If the worlds were not created, no one would grasp his eternal being in the past, present and future.

65   He is merciful, compassionate and slow to anger.

66   I speak now of *en sof*, and, with God's help, I will explain how *atsilut* and the worlds that emanate from it came to be.

67   There was at one time a great investigation and disagreement that divided the kabbalists regarding this matter.

68   It was once written that the ten *sefirot* existed in ten successive steps, each one above the other; on the other hand, it was also written that they were ordered as in lines: right, left and middle, so that the right line issues forth as *chochma, chessed, nesach* [pillar of mercy]; the left line as *bina, gevura, hod* [pillar of judgment]; and the middle as *keter, tiferet, yesod* [pillar of compassion] and *malkhut*.

69   And still there are others who are so wise as to say that the *sefirot* form concentric circles, each encircling the other.

70   The question regarding the order of the *sefirot* is deep and difficult.

71   The difference between the two different configurations
      of *sefirot* . . . is that one existed before *tikkun*; the other
      after *tikkun*.

72   *En sof* is pervasively uniform and extends infinitely with-
      out direction. It is not proper to attribute such qualities
      as "above and below," "front and back" to it. . . . The
      light of *en sof* passes through the density of each *sefira*
      and moves from the inner essence again to the outside of
      each of them in perfect totality.

73   This means: "You are a soul to my soul" as stated in the
      book of the *Zohar*.

74   And it was also written: Above all and above everything
      there is no God above nor below *en sof*. . . . And God fills
      all the worlds and moves about each side.

75   After the return of the line of light of *en sof* which was
      to be inside of the vessels, the light of Adam Kadmon's
      essence, his bones, returned and was contained inside
      of the vessels. The light remained as vessels and as the
      impression of his essence, his bones.

76   In the beginning, ten *sefirot* emanated in the image of
      circles. The circles are the ten vessels.

77   Inside each *sefira* is the essence of light called the soul.

78 The lights live on five levels: *nefesh*, *ruah*, *neshamah*, *hayah*, *yehida*.

79 Five images of light form the lower Adam.

80 This inner light is a wheel that lives inside of each vessel.

81 There is a surrounding light that moves around each vessel, as a sphere.

82 The *sefirot* live in this way, as spheres and heavens.

83 They are the heavens above our lower world.

84 The ten *sefirot* emanated in the image of straightness, as the image of man [right, left, middle]. The *sefirot* of straightness are superior to that of the circular *sefirot*.

85 The *sefirot* are in the image of the higher soul. They form the ten vessels in the image of one Adam.

86 The first ten *sefirot* of Adam Kadmon formed the image of circles called *nefesh*. Ten other sefirot of Adam Kadmon were emanated in the aspect of *ruah* of in the image of straightness as mankind, with a tall stature . . . head, arms, hands, body and legs. The line continues from *en sof* into the void and below and draws mankind with ten *sefirot* in the aspect of straightness.

87   Each of the ten vessels have an interior and an exterior. In the vessels of the ten *sefirot* are the images of bones and lights, called the higher soul.

88   In this manner are all the worlds also: The Emanated Ones, the Created Ones, the Formed Ones and Made Ones were formed in the primal space. There is nothing outside of it.

89   The light of *en sof* surrounds them and shines in all of the worlds. A great, true and real illumination spreads and permeates into every world.

90   *Ze'ir Anpin* and *Nukva* are the names of God.

91   They are spirit and their birth is hidden in the secret of divine consciousness of *Ze'ir Anpin*.

92   *Ze'ir Anpin* develops with great majesty and the *Nukva* in him are the sons of the ten full *sefirot*.

93   The *Nukva* is sawn from *Ze'ir Anpin*. *Nukva* is feminine and assumes the judgment of God; *Ze'ir Anpin* is male.

94   Thus the Tetragrammaton is called Elohim, the complete name.

95   The [feminine] Elohim is sawn from [*Ze'ir Anpin*] because beings repel Elohim.

96 The exterior worlds are vessels, body and lower soul (life force).

97 The inner worlds are the ten *sefirot* of spirit. They are formed through emanation.

98 The souls of mankind came from the man of emanation, the immanent Tetragrammaton.

99 Angels live in external worlds and they are body as well as soul.

100 The body of Elohim descends at times into the Worlds of Creation, Formation, and Making.

101 It is adorned and dressed in these clothes to coquette in front of her husband and it says: "See what I do and developments that I have made!"

102 *He* is the light that points to the returning light.

103 The upper light spreads to lower worlds. It then departs, thereby leaving a closing impression upon them.

104 The impression is that light that remains beneath when the upper light departs and disappears to its source. It exists without the upper light.

105 This remaining light became the image of a vessel. A vessel exists because the upper light spreads to it and departs.

106 It becomes a vessel in its separation from the root of its light.

107 His anger causes withdrawal of the light.

108 The measure of time in which the light does not arrive in the *sefirot* is only for one moment. . . . They exist only for a moment in his anger and because they do not have the strength to endure the [full] light.

109 But the light continues to return to lower worlds to give life.

110 The joy of the *sefirot* is to turn their faces to the light.

111 The nature of this is to give light and then to withdraw it again, as in the flame of a candle, that shakes.

112 Thus there is no measure to the span of life of the lower ones. Only through their acts will this span be determined.

113 *Chochma* is the beginning.

114 *Keter* is the upper image of the *sefirot* and is not part of the world. It is like the crown of the king that sits above the head.

115 The Rabbis said in *Sefer Yetsirah*: "He created substance from *tohu* and made that which was nothing something."

116 Before God created the four Foundations [*chochma, bina, tiferet* and *malkhut*], He created a single element of matter, called *hyly*.

117 From this *hyly*, He formed everything, brought all things into existence, clothed them and put them into their final condition.

118 This substance, which the Greeks call *hyly*, is called *tohu* in the sacred language.

119 This word was born from the expression of the sages that means: "He regretted his former deeds."

120 If a person wishes to find a name for this primordial matter, then the person might change his mind and rename it, because it is formless and can have no form to which that name should be attached.

121 The form that *tohu* ultimately assumes is called *bohu* in the sacred language.

122 One might compare this to the verse "Thou art not able *'asohu'* (to perform it)" (Ex. 18:18) and ". . . And he shall stretch over it the line of *'tohu'* and the stones of *'bohu.'*" (Is. 34:11) The stones are the forms in the building and thus constitute substance as expressed in the Hebrew *bohu*.

123 . . . *Tohu* succeeds nothingness, because there is nothing yet in it.

124 . . . He created substance from *tohu*, and made that which was nothing something. It is the thing prepared to receive the form (of the four Foundations).

125 *En sof* is called absolute zero (*efes*), because no one can conceive it. It has no matter nor form.

126 Then *tohu* came into being. It is the *keter*.

127 After *keter*, *bohu* came into being, which contains the four Foundations, *chochma*, *bina*, *tiferet* and *malkhut*.

128 There must be an intermediate point between the Emanator and the Emanated, because there is a distance between them, just as there is between Heaven and Earth.

129 But how will one illuminate the other, each of which is of two extremes?

130 How would One create the Other . . . if there were not something between them that joins them together?

131 There is such a point, near to the Emanator and near to the Emanated.

132 Behold, this point is called *keter*. It is the *tohu* and it has no Foundation in it.

133 *Keter* is the average of everything that exists between the Emanator and the Emanated.

134 There is no hint of it in the Tetragrammaton at all. It exists only at the tip of the *Yod*.

135 The *keter* is the model of all pre-matter. It is called *hyly*.

136 The *keter* contains the root of all Foundations in strength but not in actuality.

137 It is therefore called *tohu*, because one would say "There is no form in it at all." Nevertheless we see that it is emanated.

138 There are four forms in the Emanated.

139 *Keter* can be called the Emanator and the Emanated.

140 It is the greatest lower bound of all that is possible in *en sof*. Its unique emanation is the root of all the ten *sefirot*, even to the point of infinitesimally small granularity. Nothing emanated can be smaller than the *keter*. *Tohu* stands above it. There is nothing smaller than absolute zero (*efes*).

141 There are two levels. The first is the most profound lower bound of *en sof*. It receives everything from everywhere, as is known that *malkhut* receives from all of the *sefirot*.

142 From this lowest level of *en sof*, the upper level of all that exists in emanation comes into being. It contains the root of all that is emanated and emanates to all *sefirot*.

143 There is no other level between these two because the Emanator is perfectly close to Him.

144 The generality of everything is the *keter*. Its essence is of one image.

145 In the *keter* is the image of *en sof* and of the Emanated. The image of *en sof* is *Atik Yomen*.

146 *Atik Yomen* and *Arikh Anpin* are called *keter*.

147 The Emanated has only four levels. They are the four letters: *Yod, Hey, Vav, Hey*. They are the four worlds: *atsilut*, *beriah, yetsirah, asiyah.* They are *chochmah, bina, tiferet* and *malkhut.*

148 The average image between the Emanator and the Emanated is the *keter.*

149 The *keter* contains the generality of everything that is above it, although it is smaller and it depends upon everything above for sustenance.

150 In the *keter* lies the root of the ten emanated *sefirot.* The *keter* emanates in them.

151 Do not be surprised if we say the ten *sefirot* of emanation are divided into the four letters of *Yod, Hey, Vav, Hey.* They might be divided into the five *partsufim.* The ten *sefirot* are in all worlds and in all *partsufim.*

152 There is always the upper image (the Emanator) and the lower image (the Emanated).

153 Nothing that is emanated is without the letters *Yod, Hey, Vav, Hey* and the ten *sefirot.*

154 The average image among the Emanator, the Emanated, all worlds, *partsufim* and *sefirot,* is the *keter.*

155 It is clear in all of the teachings: "I am the First. And I am the Last." (Is. 44:6) The *keter* is the First and the Last.

156 *Keter* is in *malkhut* of the Emanator, which is Last. *Keter* is in the root of all that is emanated, which is the First.

157 Everything that is emanated comprises all Foundations, which are the four letters, *Yod, Hey, Vav, Hey*. They are the four worlds *atsilut, beriah, yetsirah, asiyah*.

158 Everything that was created in all worlds is of only four aspects: *Yod, Hey, Vav, Hey*. They are: breath of life (living soul), image of organs, image of coverings, image of houses. . . . The interior of all of emanation is the breath of life. It is within organs of the body, called vessels. These are the ten *sefirot*.

159 The body is the image of the ten *sefirot*. It has bounds and measure. The body is contained inside vessels of emanation. The living soul is within and has no measure at all.

160 The coverings have the aspects of houses. They are the seven palaces of emanation and are in the image of the world itself. They are: Heavens, Earth and air, in the image of houses. They are the World of Emanation inside of which sits the upper man, who is living soul and body.

161 The coverings of *malkhut* are in the palace of the upper king, who is the generality of the World of Emanation.

162 This is the image of the ten *sefirot* that issue forth from *chochma*.

163 And *keter* is the root of it all. . . . And the image of light and living soul in *keter* is the root of the ten *sefirot* of the living souls of emanation that issue forth from *chochma*.

164 The image of the palace that is in *keter* is the root of the ten *sefirot* of the palaces that are in emanation, which issue forth from *chochma*.

165 The World of Creation was made in this way, because . . . the Earth of the palace of emanation shone below.

166 The circle that surrounds all other circles is the one of *keter*. It is attached with *en sof* more than all of the rest and is most blessed. The second circle is called *chochma*. There is an interruption between it and *en sof*, which is the circle of *keter*. Consequently, the circle of *bina* is distant from *en sof* by a measure of two circles, and so on, each inside of the other, such that one is nearer to *en sof* than its associate.

167 The higher circles are more blessed than their lower associates and this continues until we find this world, the earthly material one, the midpoint, contained inside all worlds and the void. It is absolutely distant from *en sof*, more than all of the other worlds, by far. It is for this reason so much more corporeal and completely material than all other worlds, the midmost point inside of them all. And understand this well.

168 The *line* is that truest connection between the emanated circles and *en sof*.

169 Everything in the World of Emanation was sealed there. The World of Creation was called the World of Creation, because this world is the secondary light and not the upper light itself.

170 Behold there is an Emanator and what is emanated.

171 What is emanated has four Foundations: fire, breath of life, water, earth.

172 They are also the letters *Yod, Hey, Vav, Hey*.

173 They are also *chochma, bina, tiferet* and *malkhut*.

174 They are also *atsilut, beriah, yetsirah, asiyah*, of which are made the four aspects in mankind: 1. The inner man, the breath of life and soul (*nefesh*), breath of life (*ruah*), living soul (*neshamah*), spirit of life (*hayah*), individual (*yehidah*) atsilut; 2. body (*beriah*); 3. clothes that cover the body (*yetsirah*); 4. house in which man lives (*asiyah*).

175 Behold the living soul is for the living soul. And the soul is for the breath of life and the living soul. And there is the body of which bones are made and in which marrow and brains reside. And there are sinews, flesh and more.

And the Bible says: "You have clothed me with skin and flesh. And you knit me together with bones and sinews." (Job 10:11) These are the clothes and coverings.

176 What lies between the Creator and the created is the image of the breath of life.

177 A very small spark, the image of Divinity, coexists at the lowest and the highest levels in the Creator.

178 This spark is contained in the power of one created spark, the living soul, the individual. Within this soul are soul, breath of life, living soul and spirit of life.

179 It is impossible to be dressed inside of matter if not by means of something.

180 Behold the upper man has five forms, each within the other: *nefesh*, *ruah*, *neshamah*, *hayah* and *yehidah*.

181 The generality of the five forms is called the image of Adam.

182 It is not Adam himself. The five forms are called soul, spirit, life, breath, living soul. . . .

183 The generality of the vessels are substances, sinews, etc., that are called the body of mankind.

184 These generalities are in emanation (the world of *atsilut*).

185 They are likewise this way in the Worlds of Creation, Formation and Making, except that in the world of *atsilut*, all lights, images and vessels are *complete divinity*.

186 It is unique and special, as mentioned in the introduction of the *Tikkunim*: "He and his lives and his bodies are one in them. . . ." However, living soul, spirit and individual exist beyond the Worlds of Creation, Formation and Making.

187 From breath of life and below lower worlds are separated. They are called created, formed and made. All is in forms. But the images and vessels are all created, formed and made.

188 The lower man comprises all Worlds of Emanation, Creation, Formation and Making.

189 Behold, Adam's vessel was made from holiness, . . . of the dry earth of Garden of Eden, before he sinned. The vessel then became the dry earth of this world after he sinned.

190 All commandments are given so that the vessels and the images, the breath of the bone, can be repaired. They are the sparks that fell when the vessels broke.

191 The commandments were given to remove the shells from them.

192 The Image is composed of 613 limbs. All of them are from the aspect of angels that were created, formed or made.

193 These are the 613 angels who depart to the souls. These are the generalities of one image, the good inclination, which is in Adam.

194 There are 613 evil ones who are of one image, the evil inclination.

195 And in the beginning, the image was placed in the world.

196 In order to repair it, images of forms entered in it.

197 After the image was repaired, so also were the vessels.

198 After the death of Adam, who was in the vessels, his image was covered inside of other vessels, where they were truly fit for it.

199 These are called the coverings of Adam who is in the Garden of Eden of the Earth, the Upper Garden of Eden and in all worlds that lie above the Upper Garden.

200 *Neshamah* divided into some various sparks. They continued on from transmigration to transmigration.

201 The image is called the measure of the days of Adam, as
the number of his sparks is the number of the days of his
life, as mentioned in the *Zohar*, Va-yehi, p. 290.

202 And in the days that he completed the commandments,
he fixed a spark of that image. And in the days that he
had not done this, that spark of the image in respect of
that day remained defective.

203 It is in this way, therefore, that the vessels that are covered in the Garden of Eden of the Earth are repaired,
spark by spark, day by day.

204 It is impossible for the image to be covered in the vessel
unless that covering has been corrected, that is, until the
completion of its *tikkun*. It then departs this world and
goes to the Garden of Eden of the Earth and is dressed in
that central body.

205 The principle that ascends is the form that is called
Adam. The form is *yehidah*, *hayah*, *nefesh*, *ruah*, and *neshamah*. The image is also divided into five aspects. The
image covers the form. The form can not exist without
its image. The image is of good inclination and of evil

inclination. They are the angels that are in Adam, but not Adam himself. Adam is the breath of the bone that is dressed inside the vessel, the body.

206 The image is the average that spans between form and matter. Image has a likeness to both form and matter.

207 The commandments are meant to purify and clarify the image and matter. But the form is not in need of repair at all. The form did not need to be dressed in image and matter, but to continue existence in them so that they might be repaired and clarified. And understand this very well.

208 The reason that *neshamah* descended into this world was to repair and to clarify the image of the *Shekhinah* and the sparks that had fallen.

209 The angels are greater and less than *neshamah*. They are not part of the living body like Adam. They are not dressed in the body. The images of angels that accompany Adam are inferior to him because Adam is angels and form. Angels and form accompany him and are the 613 limbs of the form, his servants and chariot. Angels are the chariot for Adam and yet they are less than he. The angels of the chariot of the Holy One are higher than Adam. There are angels higher than *neshamah*.

210 These have within them aspects of matter that cover them. Body (*guf*) and vessels (*kelim*)

211 The body is divided into parts: brain (*moah*), bones (*atsamot*), sinews (*gidin*), flesh (*basar*) and skin (*or*).

212 It is impossible to dress the forms inside of a body until each is dressed inside its individual image (*tselem*).

213 There are five types of dresses compared to the five forms. There are the images of *nefesh*, *ruah*, *neshamah*, *hayah* and *yehidah*.

214 The five dresses of the five forms are images and they are in the secret of the 288 sparks that remained inside the vessels that were broken. They are called breath of the bone.

215 They are the sparks from the Tetragrammaton.

216 It was necessary that the Holy One, blessed be He, create his world and set his world into the world: Everything is in contrast of the brain to the belly. . . . Each world is formed in this fashion. He covers the belly, moving from world to world, covering each belly, going round each one.

217 And though it might appear that the innermost part of each world is the brain and that which covers it is the

shell, this is not so. If you expand your intellect, you will understand that we are speaking of the worth of each of us who dwell upon the lower Earth, this Earth that cleaves so near to everyone below. It is the aspect of the shell that encircles our value and worth, in contrast to the brain that is above it. The brain is the circle that goes round the Earth, followed by subsequent circles extending upwardly, each exceeding our own value more and more. Each higher circle is the brain to the lower, extending on to *en sof*, which lies above and within everything that is emanated.

218 *En sof* is the brain that is above all. All that is emanated forms shells that envelop it.

219 The circle nearest lower Earth is the outermost of all shells from *en sof*.

All circles are in the image of shells.

220 Each world, on the other hand, sees the shell that goes round the brain and views things differently.

221 Adam is drawn is straightness and some worlds are comprised within him.

222 The Tetragrammaton is split into pieces, existing in successive steps.

They form one body. . . . The worlds drawn in the image of Adam form one world.

223 All images are drawn in the image of Adam. They are the brain to the belly, the higher image over each belly, successively. *Atik Yomen* is to the belly of *Arikh Anpin*; *Arikh Anpin* is to the belly of *Abba* and *Ima*; *Abba* and *Ima* are to the belly of *Ze'ir Anpin* and *Nukva*, etc. The ten *sefirot* follow likewise in successive steps.

224 Each is in contrast to the belly of the other; this one the brain, the other the shell (belly).

225 It is in this way that the one emanating became attached to that which was emanated.

226 All worlds are contained in him. We do not have permission to speak of the inner essence of this man. We only speak about what he emanates.

227 We now explain withdrawal of the upper light.

228 Upper light spreads, then disappears and returns to its source. It leaves a closing impression below after it has departed.

229 The impression of light that remains below when the upper light returns to its source is the remaining light.

This makes the aspect of a vessel. The spread of light and its subsequent disappearance cause the existence of vessels.

230 The light arrives and does not arrive. It is written in the *Zohar*.

231 You should not think that the ten *sefirot* are superior and beyond all that was emanated, because other worlds are above them. They were not considered because they were not visible and they are hidden in a wondrous secret. Let your eyes see. There are three articles in the book of *Tikkunim* that discuss the many worlds that are obscured within the *sefirot*. . . . And if you apply your intellect well to the many hints and esoterica among these articles, you will be amazed and astonished when you see how many levels upon levels without number preceded the four Foundations, worlds and ten *sefirot* of emanation.

232 The scholars hid these things in the sweetness of their language and called them the "ten burnishments above the upper *keter*" and other such things.

233 There is no end to the worlds in these places, because there are thousands and tens of thousands and so on.

234 There is one entity that is included in all worlds and places. All worlds develop from it, depend on it and grasp into it. They exit from it and are revealed as sepa-

rate entities from it. This entity is Adam Kadmon. Adam Kadmon preceded all.

235 In the great ascents and hidden power of Adam Kadmon, one did not discuss the secret of what was revealed in some hidden places. . . . I will mention some of them. In the *Tikkunim* at the end of Tikkun 19, p. 41b is written: "Shall we say . . . It is known that Adam Kadmon exists for all that preceded everything? And is there yet another Adam?"

236 The *Tikkunim* says: "A great craftsman made a drawing in the palace of Adam Kadmon for everything that preceded. That drawing is Adam."

237 The *Zohar* says: "The king has brought me into his chambers." This means that the twenty-two letters of the Hebrew alphabet spread and illuminate from the very beginning of illumination and you already knew that the beginnings of the king were established in grace and strength.

238 *Malkhut* has no cause because it is the image of the lower soul, the force of life.

239 The ten *sefirot* of *atsilut* are divided into five aspects, which are: *Arikh Anpin, Abba, Ima, Ze'ir Anpin* and *Nukva*. All have the generality of one Adam. All move within one thought, as Adam's limbs move within one thought.

240 The world of *atsilut* is called thought just as the substance and life of *en sof* are one in unity and this thought indeed moves inside of *atsilut*.

241 Everything is truly one thing.

242 It and its substance are one because it is with everything together. It is not the case that thought precedes action, because everything becomes one.

243 In the *Zohar*, Parashat Pekude, p. 262 it is written that thought, will of the heart, voice and speech make the four worlds: *atsilut, beriah, yetsirah, asiyah*.

244 *Abba* is called thought and it can not be comprehended . . . *bina* is *Nukva*. It has the power to form vessels. Within life, *bina* is closest to matter.

Bina is *leshon banyan*, which means the dialectic of building.

245 *Neshamah*, the higher soul, has ten complete *sefirot*. It is the countenance within *Ze'ir Anpin* of the World of Emanation.

246 We now speak of secrets. We know that when *Ima* emanates inside of *Ze'ir Anpin*, it is as a mother who sits upon her young. If *Abba* wishes to join with *Ima*, he lowers his head toward her so that they might be together. . . . The

child that forms from their union is born in the image of divine consciousness. And all of *Zeir's* and *Nukva's* children inherit it so that they will join and finally give birth to new higher souls for the children of Adam.

247 Only within the union of their divine consciousness do *Zeir* and *Nukva* truly give birth to *Neshamot*, which is given to them by *Abba* and *Ima*.

248 Pure divine consciousness makes the birth of souls possible.

249 No birth can unfold without divine consciousness, *Abba* and *Ima*. They are true divine consciousness.

250 *Abba* and *Ima* . . . join together. Their crowns and inner consciousness are inherited by the children of *Zeir* and *Nukva* of creation.

251 *Zeir* and *Nukva* give birth to *Neshamot* of the angels of *yetsirah*, because the dwelling place of angels is in *yetsirah*.

252 All sacred union serves the young. . . . It serves in their conception, birth, nursing and development.

253 It is called divine inner consciousness. It comes from *Abba* and *Ima* of *atsilut*. The upper matings of *Abba* and *Ima* of *atsilut* serve *Abba* and *Ima* of *beriah* so that they

will, in turn, give divine consciousness to *Zeir* and *Nukva*, who, in turn, will give birth to souls of new angels.

254 There are two aspects of divine union between *Ze'ir Anpin* and *Nukva* of *atsilut*. They are either united, [face to face] or unconscious and joined [back to back].

255 Before Adam was created and before the creation of the world, *Zeir* and *Nukva* were unconscious and joined [back to back]. Therefore, all worlds were unconscious and joined according to this secret in the World of Making. Our world existed in this same state.

256 Divine inner consciousness is the vessel of the soul. The heart is the vessel of the soul's higher emotions and the liver is the vessel of its physical life-force. The soul spreads from divine consciousness throughout the body. . . . it is called adult *Ze'ir Anpin*, the divine inner consciousness. . . . It is recognized only in this consciousness and not in the body.

257 The soul's higher emotions spread from within the heart and into the body. The heart is the intermediate vessel that is called nursing . . . and it is the garment for the upper soul and divine consciousness. The upper soul is only recognized in divine consciousness because the body is no longer perceived. Then the soul's physical life force spreads inside of the liver. It covers the soul's higher

emotions and heart. The soul's higher emotions are only recognized in the heart.

258 This is therefore the order of their roots and very essence. You understand now how all of the World of Emanation moves in understanding that flows into form (*bina*) and *bina* is its higher soul. Half of it is exposed and half of it is hidden in *Ze'ir Anpin* who is the soul's higher emotions. Half of it is exposed and half of it is hidden in *Nukva* who is the soul's physical life-force.

259 The vessel of divine consciousness moves throughout all of the body.

260 Behold there are three vessels, each contained within the other. They are in the images of *ibur* (conception), *yenikah* (nursing) and *mohin* (divine consciousness). They are vessels for the soul's physical life force, higher emotions and upper levels. . . .

261 Then the flesh [red fire] covers them. This is called red flesh. This is the secret of the electrum that surrounds the vessels. ". . . as the color of electrum, out of the midst of the fire . . ." (Ez. 1:4) And this is the secret of red flesh. Then there is the skin. And it is the Tree of Knowledge, the good that is in *atsilut*. And behold flesh is the name Elohim that surrounds living forms and it is called the Throne of Sparks.

262 *Ze'ir Anpin, Nukva* and all creatures are the children of *Abba* and *Ima*. And we, his nation, Israel, are all created by *Zeir* and *Nukva*. We are their children. . . . Imperfection of the children reaches back to the parents, who are *Zeir* and *Nukva*.

263 Behold, external forces and matter rule only in *Ze'ir Anpin* and *Nukva*.

264 They are called the seven days of Genesis in which the world was created.

265 Angry God will vanquish and subjugate the *kelipot*.

266 . . . We have explained the matter of the *Shekhinah* in Exile. Adam ha-Rishon sinned and mixed good in evil. And the souls of holiness fell into the *kelipot*. And there is no strength in them to leave it, were it not because of His mercy, may he be blessed. And this gives Him sorrow. And the *Shekhinah* of His strength goes with Israel in Exile inside the *kelipot*. It enters in their place and gathers those souls from there.

267 It was necessary to create one Adam, who would be part of all created and emanated ones, who ties all worlds together, until the depth of the Earth. He is nearest to receive the emanation from the ten *sefirot*. And then, in the *tikkun* of his deeds, he would draw the emanation

from the ten *sefirot* to himself, and from himself to the angels, and from them to the *kelipot*, in order that it would be repaired, [. . . .] and from it to the worlds themselves that make vessels and the forms of letters of each word.

268 It was necessary that mankind would be composed from all the worlds, so that these worlds might help mankind in his deeds and continue the flow of emanation to him and from him to the worlds again in return, because the worlds do not have the strength to sustain emanations without mankind's participation. And therefore when man sins all the worlds are spoiled and receive punishment and a lessening of emanation in themselves, because they did not help mankind.

269 In the beginning, the Emanator formed vessels from his own profound absence.

He withdrew all light to the highest regions because judgments and vessels can only be revealed during the absence of *en sof*. Sacred light abrogates that which is to be created. And therefore vessels would not hypostasize and would efface completely because of the abundance of emanation of *en sof*.

270 And their spirit, the lights and essence shining in them, ascended from whence they came, to Elohim, the Upper Mother. And therefore, it is called death.

271 Their souls—their lights—ascended to their first place, which is emanation.

272 The measure of judgement always limits grace, so that it does not increase, like the vessel limits water so that it does not spread outside. This is the essential meaning of the vessels.

273 The root of evil comes from the broken vessels. Good comes from the great light. And if it were not so, there would be only good in the world.

274 The intention of *en sof* is to develop the worlds below such that the lower world would be separated at a distance from *en sof* more than the upper world that is above it. Thus, world after world in succession is made distant from *en sof* in its own measure of distance and separation, so that judgment would be revealed and come into being, level after level, until the last waste of these drosses that is contained in all of the worlds and in *asiyah* would be purified.

275 The light which comes by way of returning above is the light returning and it is judgment.

276 Behold the Emanator, may his name be blessed, made this lower Earth from the generality of the worlds of *atsilut, beriah, yetsirah, asiyah*. These worlds are in his people

of Israel, whom he has chosen so that they might connect these four worlds together here below.

277 When a person is born, the soul of that person must purify the sparks that fell to his or to her share. The sparks fell because of the sin of Adam ha-Rishon in *Kelipah Nogah.* This is why a person is born into this world.

278 When the lower ones have the strength and completeness to accept the upper light of the Emanator, then the upper lights yearn to shine below. And the lights turn their faces below toward those who wish to receive them and these faces shine upon their faces. And when completeness is lacking in the lower ones, the lights ascend and turn their faces toward the Emanator, because it is their wish to return there. And they turn their backs toward the lower ones. The new illumination shines by way of their backs upon the lower ones. And the lower ones receive the illumination, which is necessary for their life and not more. And behold the first light, which descends below, is straight and merciful. It is called the light of the face. The light that departs upwardly to the Emanator is called the returning light, the light of the back, judgment. . . . This light emanated without his will is called sustaining, exterior female light."

279 The ten *sefirot* do not require deeds. As emanation makes them arise, they accept their divine potential and flow

into emanation. *En sof* draws emanation continually to them. It is said of *en sof*: For thou art not a God that has pleasure in wickedness. Evil will not sojourn with you.

280 The kings ascend with them. The kings enter in, according to the secret of *mayin nukvin*. They are then purified by the *mayin dekhurin*. Then, the kings come to this world in lower bodies, as the souls of Israel.

Adam among the Worlds

1   Adam is part of all of the worlds.

2   Every world participated in his making. His image is within each of them. The worlds are able to exist through his actions.

3   Humanity's actions make life flow to Heaven and to Earth. It is as if mankind created them both.

4   Adam was not of the material world and was dressed in light.

5   He was comprised of all souls that were part of the 6000 years that would be the world. His limbs were made from these souls. When he sinned, they vanished from him because shells—external forces—took control of him.

6   The remnants of these souls shed from him and fell into the depths of shells (matter). Souls are controlled by matter because of the sin of Adam.

7   When the souls that were in Adam fell into the shells and external forces, they mingled among the four winds of the world and took his dust. Each of the seventy Officers of the nations of the world is trapped in the realm of matter and took his part from Adam.

8   Angry God stops external forces and subjugates their power.

9   Adam lived in holiness in the World of Creation. The World of Creation is made from the soil of the Garden of Eden of the Earth.

10   This soil consists of the soul's physical life force, its most upper levels and its higher emotions.

11   After Adam sinned, all worlds descended from their place of holiness. The World of Forming descended and clothed itself in the World of Making. . . . The World of Creation descended and clothed itself in the World of Forming. *Nukva* descended to the World of Creation and clothed herself therein. *Ze'ir Anpin* descended and clothed himself in *Nukva*.

12   Adam's body was from the World of Forming, but only
his spirit resides there now. His existence is strewn
among various levels. And his body and lower soul are
now in this world, the World of Making. These things
caused much spoilage among the worlds.

13   Evil and Good are equal in the World of Making . . .
External powers grasp there. The faces of God are broken
there . . . evil prevails over good.

14   If Adam had not sinned, all worlds would have been
repaired and sustained in union and divine consciousness.

15   Shells existed before the sin of Adam. They were in
the four Worlds of Emanation, Creation, Formation
and Making. Let us explain what Adam caused in these
worlds after his sin.

16   Behold, before the creation of the world, the World of
Emanation was broken.

17   After it was repaired, lower worlds were still broken,
devoid of reparation and atonement.

18   Adam repaired most of the worlds. He restored their
unity and consciousness.

19   But Adam could not repair the World of Making, where evil rules. This world is not conscious, yet it lives. There are many external forces and much evil in it. The waste is far greater than the food. There is much grasping of the external ones. They are strange gods. These strange gods are gods who are trapped among the external forces in the World of Making.

20   The globe of this lower Earth upon which people, domesticated and wild animals live exists in the aspect of vessels. It is called the World of Making. It is the most exterior of all of the worlds. . . . They surround the Heavens which are above this Earth.

21   . . . . The World of Separation is of the lower worlds and is godless. . . . These worlds are called Tree of Knowledge that is both good and evil. *Shekhinah* is in a state of lessening. She descends and clothes herself inside of them. *Shekhinah* is called Tree of Knowledge that is both good and evil. When she descends, her feet go down to death. This is where death is found, among the shells and coverings.

22   The active, divine presence in our world is divided into ten *sefirot*. They form seven Earths, each Earth above the other. Between each Earth is a Heaven. They form the secret of surrounding lights that are in each world. . . . Each Earth is one Adam. Each has a mouth, ears, navel,

pudenta, etc. The Foundation that is in each Earth receives emanations from the Earth that is directly above it. The Foundation is the land of Israel.

23 The Earth is a garment of the divine presence. Sitra Ahara surrounds it.

24 Coverings are the most external part of Creation. They are the four Foundations of fire, breath of life, water and earth. These Foundations are called the Posterior Ones of the World of Making. The shells grasp into these coverings. The coverings are called other gods. Earth is completely holy. Sitra Ahara is completely unclean.

25 Shells grasp into the skin, where the trapped sparks lie. The skin has inner brightness and light from the 288 sparks of the Kings of Edom. It awaits to be purified. . . . Evil influences attempt to attach themselves to *Zeir* and *Nukva*. The power of inner brightness protects them. When there is sin, it departs, leaving only naked skin. There is a spark of holiness in the interior of the skin. . . . The skin itself remains evil . . . just as the shells. The shells nurse from this flesh.

26 *Ze'ir Anpin* emanates in *Nukva*, and they join in sacred unity. But shells suck and grasp into the skin of her womb and entice *Ze'ir Anpin's* emanation so that it changes into desire for her flesh. The desire draws itself to the

external world. Shells make *Ze'ir Anpin* turn away from holiness to desire and changes his pure emanation into discharges of semen.

27   Let us explain the matter of our world. Behold, the Heavens that we see with our eyes are the ten circles that are in our world. And in the midst of the circles of this vacuum, the upright body of inner divine presence spreads out among them. The body of divine presence is the Garden of Eden of our Earth. Upon her back is skin. Upon the back of the skin are shells. Around the shells are her garments, surrounding lights and the Heavens. This is Jerusalem! I have set her in the midst of the nations. The active, divine presence of this world is Jerusalem. Shells, evil, and the seventy Officers surround her, as mentioned in the *Zohar*, Parashat Va-yakhel, p. 209. . . . The Garden of Eden of the Earth is very pure and holy material. Around it is pure matter, where external forces and shells rule. In it are coarse dregs of matter and shells and no greater coarseness like it exists. All worlds and higher palaces of holiness strive to purify this thick coarseness of matter that clings to the Garden of Eden of the Earth.

28   The shells seek to give the Earth thickness. Therefore, deeds of this world are harsh and evil. The wicked prevail.

29   The names of God are found in every *sefira*. Each *sefira* would say: "Behold, you have found the names of God in minerals, silver, gold, precious stones, rocks, rivers, mountains, hills and in all remaining palaces, such as houses, fields and grounds. In them are all types of minerals, as well in the ten *sefirot* of the palaces. And everything is as it should be. In this way, there are many names of God in these forms and coverings. There are many names of God in all limbs. And all of these things are truly present for anyone who seeks them.

30   In the *Zohar*, Parashat Terumah, p. 144, it is written: "In this world that gleams and shines, Sitra Ahara entices Eve, because he cleaves in her in the secret of foreskin, which is the evil that is in the skin of *Nukva*. He nurses from the powers of Holiness."

31   When Israel sins, God forbid, the Upper Mother departs from her children. Then shells are able to nurse from the inner light of *Zeir* and *Nukva*. Understand the secret of the Upper Mother who must abandon her children when Israel sins.

32   The soul of the World of Emanation could reside in Adam and allow him to ascend higher. And if he would attain the breath of life from the aspect of the

Foundation of this world, then he would be the husband of the Matronita. And Adam would be called Ish Elohim (Man of Elohim).

33   Just as a righteous person's soul ascends in the secret of sacred female waters within God in our world, there are also other souls that ascend in the secret of male waters in God. But there has been no spiritual mating since the destruction of the temple and there is no gardener to sow the seed. His garden grows over with aftergrowths that now spring forth.

34   The aftergrowths are the living souls of righteous people who developed and left the upper garden of God in our world. They now return so that they might ascend in sacred emanations of female and male waters. It is written in the secret: Light is sown for the righteous. And gladness is for the upright in heart, which was always sown from the beginning. And we sow it now anew. (Ps. 97:11 and Parashat Terumah, p. 166b)

35   Mankind was given the good inclination, the evil inclination and the higher soul. The light of the angels is called the good inclination. The light from the light of the shells is called the evil inclination and lies outside of the good. The higher soul is the innermost part of mankind. It is the innermost part because it is called the bones, the essence, of mankind. Mankind therefore has free will to do what it wishes because it is greater than

this. Mankind's major inclination is the good inclination because it is holy and because it is very akin to the good inclination. The body possesses the major share of the evil inclination. It is akin to evil and associates closely with other bodies so that it might fulfill its needs.

36   Mankind was created from all of the worlds. In this way, each world helps mankind with good deeds and brings the flow of emanations to mankind and mankind returns them back to the worlds again in return. This is necessary because the worlds do not have the strength to sustain emanations without mankind's help. Therefore, when a person sins, all of the worlds are spoiled. They receive punishment and their emanations become weaker because they did not help mankind.

37   There is a unique light called the World of the Ten Sefirot. This world is in the form of mankind. There is also another light called the World of Higher Souls of the sons of Adam and it is part of all of the aspects of Adam and the ten *sefirot*.

38   There is another light in the form of Adam called the World of Angels.

39   One small light remains. It is called the dark light. It consists of harsh judgments and severity. All shells from all worlds emanate from it and it forms the outer garment of the World of Angels. The dark light is also in the

image of Adam. And outside of all of these lights are the firmaments themselves that are around all of the worlds. They are the body that curves around each world. Inside of these worlds are five lights: the light of *en sof*, the innermost light; further outward is the light of the ten *sefirot*; then further is the World of Higher Souls; next is the World of Angels; and above all of these worlds are the firmaments, called the body of all lights.

40   The body of dry earth is in the World of Making. It is the lowly world. Inside of it is the basic soul in the aspect of shells. Inside of this is the image of angels of this world. They help plants and the like to grow. Inside of this is the aspect of higher souls of the sons of mankind.

41   They are made from a chariot of light drawn by the lights of the ten *sefirot* in the World of Making. The World of Making is inside of the four Foundations so that they might have life. These *sefirot* are inside of everything. And therefore, the Wheel of Making and the three worlds of Formation, Creation and Emanation act within mankind.

42   The world of the upper souls is innermost and highest of that of all of the angels. The angels are their servants. They draw their light and life in their service from the light of the ten *sefirot*. This is in the secret: "Behold their valiant ones cry without. The ambassadors of peace weep

bitterly." (Is. 33:7) If emanation is not drawn from the ten *sefirot* to the souls of Israel, they will lack emanation and the exterior ones continue to stand above them.

43   Even the higher souls of innermost worlds do not have the strength to withstand the shells. The Nefilim that had descended were consumed by the world below and will be wiped out in the Time to Come.

44   Higher souls are very great. Higher souls are lights in birth that flow from the ten *sefirot*.

45   Behold, the light of the higher souls is a garment for the light of the ten *sefirot*. And this is the secret: "My beloved is gone down to his garden, to the bed of spices, to feed in the gardens and to gather lilies." (Song of Songs 6:2) He picks the higher souls of the righteous from this garden because of the fragrance that shines through their deeds in this world. When He picks them, they will be dressed in their light. And this is the secret: "But you that did cleave unto the Lord your God are alive everyone of you this day." (Deut. 4:4) This is complete connection with the light of the ten *sefirot*. But this is not entirely so in creation. It is written: ". . . I have caused the houses of Israel and Judah to cleave unto me, said the Lord. That they might be unto me for a people, and for a name, and for a praise, and for a glory. But they would not hearken." (Jerem. 13:11)

46 Divine inner presence has several forms. Lower soul possesses the aspect of the masculine, so that its divine presence will arouse sacred female waters. Emanations then join together. In this way, the lower soul becomes a vessel. . . . Then the higher and highest levels of soul awake. . . . The souls of the righteous join in emanations with this divine presence and through their union more higher souls are made.

47 *En sof* shines in all of the worlds in two fashions: from the inside and from the outside. It surrounds all the worlds from the outside. Adam Kadmon is the inner light and he is contained in all of the worlds. The light of *en sof* is internal and external. Inner light departs; surrounding light goes within. All worlds sustain their existence in this way.

48 The upper worlds are one holy entity. They are one Divinity and undifferentiated. . . . The three lower Worlds of Creation, Formation and Making are aspects of this Divinity and are found only in the higher soul.

49 There are an infinite number of angels. The holy names of all the Pentateuch comprise the name of the Holy One.

50 *Bina* is the flaming sword, which lashes toward every direction with mercy and judgment so that the righteous might receive their reward in the world to come. The

Shekhinah is the flaming sword, which does likewise upon this Earth so that it might bring judgment to the wicked.

51   The divine inner presence of our world . . . is the flaming sword for the wicked.

52   Jerusalem's right arm is to the south; her left, to the north; her face, to the east; her back is to the west and her head is to the Heavens which are the nine *sefirot* above her.

53   Therefore, Adam was created male and faces the east; his back was created female and she faces the west. And this is the secret: the *Shekhinah* is in the west.

54   Even this very Earth is inside of the inner light, the Holy Temple. Opposite the Earth is uncleanliness of the exterior ones. They are demons found in the likes of toilets and rivers. The Earth itself is a garment, as is written: "They shall perish. However, you shall endure. Yea, all of them shall wax old like a garment. As a vesture shall you change them. And they shall pass away." (Ps. 102:27) This is because the exterior limbs are the lands of the seventy nations and air, seas and oceans that surround them. The inner limbs are the land of Israel, the Holy Temple and the Holy of Holies.

55   The essence of the earthly Garden of Eden arises out of external forces and grasping from everywhere. . . . Adam

caused the snake to enter into the Tree of Knowledge. And when he touched it, the Tree shouted: "Evil one, do not touch me." The fruit that stands opposite the mother is the Tree of Life, seventy palm trees, seventy branches, twelve springs, twelve tribes. And the remaining trees in the Garden are the *sefirot* that are there. It is written: "And the Lord God commanded the man and said: 'Of every tree of the garden, you may freely eat.'" (Gen. 1:16)

56 The twenty-two letters of the Hebrew alphabet of the Torah are rooted in the firmament that exists in the secret of knowledge. . . . The Upper Dew is drawn from the inner consciousnesses of the Ancient Holy One and is given to *Ze'ir Anpin*. From his mind are formed the twenty-two letters in this sacred knowledge. . . . From *Ze'ir Anpin* food descends to souls to bring their being forth into the Garden of Eden on the Earth. The Torah is the food. Commandments are the garments.

57 Within this firmament, the secret of knowledge, one pillar forms. It is in the image of the spinal column that descends from this knowledge to its Foundation. . . . It continues downward until it meets the ground of the Garden. The Ground is divine inner presence. Within this presence souls ascend and descend frequently. There are three colors of the rainbow in it. The Foundation is comprised of grace, severity and harmony, as three colors. The root of each soul ascends in the image of one such

color. . . . During the time of mating. . . . The highest souls ascend in the secret of female waters to this firmament which is called the knowledge of *Nukva*. These souls receive holy emanations of male waters. They shine together in blissful unity. This is the greatest pleasure that is so often mentioned in the *Zohar*.

58 The World to Come and the Future . . . are in *Ima*. Tevunah is the lower level of the *Shekhinah* and reflects discernment in mankind. Tevunah enters into the back of Ze'ir Anpin's head as divine consciousness and she is called the World to Come. . . . The World of Tevunah is always coming in the secret visage of divine consciousness. As it was written in *Sefer ha-Bahir*: "His pupils asked, 'What is the World to Come?' He said to them: 'A world that has already come.'" The explanation is that it is continual and has already come into the head of Ze'ir Anpin and will always continue to do so. The World to Come is as its translation into Aramaic, Alma di-ati (World that comes). And the explanation is that it comes frequently and is continued in the head of Ze'ir Anpin. Bina, aspect of the intellect, however, is called the Time to Come, in Aramaic, Le-Atid la-vo, (that which still did not come). Certainly these things will come afterward and increase the ascent of Ze'ir Anpin. And then there will always be divine consciousness from *bina* for him, but it will not always come from Tevunah. And this is the meaning of the saying: Le-Atid la-vo "In the Time to Come."

59   All of the worlds have the generality of the face of mankind. They are the face of mankind in substance, vessels, and coverings everywhere.

60   In each of the worlds are: soul, life-force, higher emotions, higher soul, life and highest soul. The worlds have bodily limbs, called vessels.

61   The soul's highest level and life itself are the surrounding ones. They are not vessels. The soul's life force, higher emotions and higher levels are within and do not surround.

62   A dream is not from the lower soul, the life force. It is from the higher soul of the breath of life that gives the body life because the soul of a person comes from the four Foundations.

63   The chair of Ezekiel is in the World of Formation. . . . Inner light and surrounding light are in all worlds. The vessels interrupt these worlds such that lights are within them and lights surround them. Inner lights and their vessels are uppermost and outer lights are lowermost. The Ancient Holy One is within. His vessel is contained in all. Next, is the inner light and vessel of the Patient One. This inner presence continues down to the World of Making. This world's inner light and vessel cloak all other worlds.

64   Fire, hail, snow, vapor and stormy wind are in the World of Emanation and fulfill His word. Skin makes the shell. Shells have three forms: cloud, stormy wind and fire, as three uncircumcised membranes: the membrane itself; splitting of the membrane and pulling it down; dripping blood. Inside of all of them is flesh and corona of the membrane. The brightness surrounds the shell. (Ez. 1.4 "A brightness was round about it.") The fourth form of shells is: ". . . and after the earthquake, a fire. But the Lord was not in the fire. And after the fire a still small voice. (I Kings 19:12) The brightness is the power in living creatures that speak fire in silence. It is the Tree of Knowledge and the good of the world of *atsilut*, as is mentioned in the *Tikkunim*, p. 30.

65   The Tree of Knowledge, both good and evil, is in the Worlds of Creation, Formation and Making, but the brightness is not evil. Glowing shells surround or interrupt the brightness that lives in the matter. Matter is good and evil in these worlds. It is all good in the world of *atsilut*.

66   You must know that every aspect of the worlds is akin to shells and vessels. . . . Glowing accompanies shells and vessels, the shell of the skin. . . .

67   Glowing is Batyah, daughter of Pharoah. Pharoah sent a mixed multitude that came from the glowing shells, they are like Lilith, the stiff-necked one, the garment of Eve, wife of Adam. There is a greater exterior Lilith. She is the wife of Samael. She is also in this glowing. There are other inner Samaels and Liliths. Our scholars said that the inner Samaels and Liliths are an angel who was banished from Heaven. He is called: ". . . the flaming sword, which turned every way . . . ," (Gen. 3:24) at times he is angel, at times he is a demon. It is also called Lilith, since *Nukva* rules at night, as is mentioned in the *Tikkunim*, p. 124.

68 Samael and Lilith are the three exterior forms of matter. There are many Samaels and Liliths. They enticed Adam and Eve.

69 This glowing mingled in Adam and Eve. Then Adam and Eve were made good and evil.

70 It is written in Parashah va-yehi 221 and Va-hakhel, 203: "The Sitra Ahara entices the wife in this glowing. . . ," because Adam and Eve are the divine consciousness that is inside of the shells. The shells are separated from this consciousness. Shells and divine consciousness adhere to each other, as light permeates matter and glows through it.

71 Every transgression below causes a transgression above. So *Ze'ir Anpin* desired the *Nukva* and he roared throughout his dwelling place. And as he treated her in this way above in the world of *atsilut*, she was forced into exile,

below in the World of Creation. So a soul leaves and goes below into exile because the male's desire is not answered in turn by that of the female's desire. Hence by chance a bad maid springs forth in the secret: "A maid will inherit her mistress." She takes her soul. You must understand the extent of severity that a transgression above inflicts upon those who live below.

72 Glowing couches closely to deceit and to evil.

73 Glowing couches closely to deceit and to evil. Divine inner presence cleaves to truth and to the soul. The glowing turns from mercy to judgment as it changes itself. . . . Glowing only imitates the likeness of the ten *sefirot*.

74 The *Shekhinah* wishes to feed the Exterior Ones in the secret: ". . . and his kingdom rules over all." (Ps. 103:19) She gives sustenance by means of glowing shells. It was written: "It was dyed in this color in order to feed them."

75 Glowing shells are the hide of the serpent. They are the outer shells that comprise all such worlds. The snake is within them and they are mixed with holiness. The shells of storm (stormy wind, Ez. 1:4) are the inner life of the snake. The snake has an inner world . . . Stormy wind surges below, then strives to ascend. . . . Glowing is the highest and lives within all of them. Glowing is near to holiness. It is called the hide of the snake in the *Tikkunim* 36.

76   There are two angels. One is called the good inclination, the other is called the evil inclination. The good and evil inclinations are the guardians of mankind and they advise mankind for its own good. In some places it is said that the good inclination is an angel and the evil inclination is a demon. The Tree of Knowledge is hidden in knowledge. It has grace and severity in it. Grace and severity are holiness and they are good. But when exterior forces nurse from the Tree, it mingles with good and evil. In the beginning, severities spread throughout *Ze'ir Anpin's* body before the graces began to spread. But because of Adam's sin, knowledge descended below, between Adam's shoulders. While it was between his two shoulders, severity then followed and descended to there as well. . . . Because severity descended before graces, they could not be sweetened by them. This is one defect. The second defect is that severity spread throughout the body of *Ze'ir Anpin.* Graces have not yet spread into his body. External forces grasp into it. The third defect is that the graces are naked and exposed to grasping of external forces. External forces desire to grasp into severity but they also grasp into the graces as well.

77   When a human being is born, its soul must purify the sparks that it inherited. These sparks fell to him because of the sin of Adam and the reason that a human being is born in this world is to purify them.

78   The father and the mother are blessed because they draw a soul from above to the fetus according to the commandments of man and woman. The root of their higher soul is similar. Through their actions, they purify some of the sparks of the glowing shells that clothes the soul of the fetus. But that soul is still in the image of a fetus and there is still no knowledge in it. The image of the fetus can be repaired through the purity and goodness of the deeds of the father and the mother.

79   When the child is born, the evil inclination enters into it immediately. . . . The divine consciousnesses of nursing enter into the child. They are called Elohi. . . . The evil inclination entered first because of the second defect caused by Adam. That is, as divine consciousness entered and was expanding in *Ze'ir Anpin*, severities descended first. Therefore evil inclinations and severities descended first and grasped into mankind as well. Therefore, male children are circumcised in order to remove this evil, i.e., the uncircumcised membrane of childhood that clings while the child yet nurses. Then the child will have knowledge and it will descend to his foundation, to his *yesod*, below his waist. . . .

80   The shells of glowing possess the will and the way to make garments for the soul, to capture it and to exploit it. This is the secret of the hide of the snake. It loves to

dress the clean soul. The upper souls are clean and have garments of light. Hekhal VII. *Atsilut, beriah, yetsirah, asiyah, shaar.* (Gate 49) *Kitsur, atsilut, beriah, yetsirah, asiyah,* Perek 3, p. 397.

81   It is possible that humanity might not be able to repair its own soul during the days apportioned to it, because it did not complete the commandments that said that it must purify its garment that is trapped in the glowing. Then the soul will not be able to enter.

82   When male and female mate, take special care, because it is written: "If you do well, shall it not be lifted up? And if you do not do well, sin couches at the door. And unto you is its desire, but you can rule over it." (Gen. 4:7) You must understand that the garment and the body are the evil inclination. . . . The garment is made for *nefesh* from severities and they are in the glowing shells and the glowing shells are the evil inclination because they have not yet been purified. These things are full of shells and dregs. . . . However when the good inclination, the garment of graces comes, the glowing shells exit forthwith. Evil does not rule there, because they are the graces.

83   When the good inclination enters, it sweetens the evil inclination. The evil inclination changes from demon to angel. There are two angels who watch over a person because the severity that had been there previously has been changed and serves as a good angel.

84 Morning dawns and evening dusks in the secret: "She rises while it is yet night and gives food to her household and a portion of it to her maidens. She is hidden from the day and is only revealed during the night." (Prov. 31:15) Behold, the three Worlds of Creation, Formation and Making are complete vessels, but not divinity. They are therefore called seals of emanation. The breath of life of the life force and higher, upper souls come from vessels of emanation. They shine their seals, their impressions, upon these three worlds. They then become complete vessels for life force, higher and upper souls.

85 Jerusalem is the *Nukva* of *Ze'ir Anpin*. She was destroyed, yet she continued. . . .

86 The Emanator, may his name be blessed, gave the lower Earth the same generalities as those of the upper Worlds of Emanation, Creation, Formation, and Making. The gifts of the upper worlds live below in the people of Israel . . . they will join all upper worlds together as they live here on Earth. The people of Israel strive to have the strength needed to purify sins in the Tree of Knowledge, good and evil, according to the aspects of the four upper worlds.

87 The body of this world is the ground and its minerals. The ground is the exterior vessel and it surrounds all of the inner lights. . . . The ground possesses all vegetation and it is the vessel of the breath, the soul. Animals possess the higher soul. Then there is wilderness, the vessel of life. These are the four Foundations: ground, vegetation, animals, and wilderness.

88 These things signify the four elements of life: water, fire, breath of life, dust. Behold the demons and evil spirits that are found in this Earth. They are the exterior shells.

89 Just as there is holiness, there are also higher souls of the children of mankind and they come from the interior worlds. Higher souls and angels also come from the exterior worlds. Higher souls from the good inclination and evil inclination exit from within the Tree of Knowledge that lives in the glowing shells. Angels and demons that are appointed over the workers of the world and its stars and constellations enter the Tree from the outside. These are the exterior demons of this world and they are called the evil inclination of the sons of mankind.

90 The most excellent part of glowing shells that lay within the vessels ascends on the Sabbath and takes additional soul. Then the garment of a person's soul that comes from good and evil inclinations of glowing shells ascends as well and dresses in another higher soul. . . . In this way all might receive additional soul.

91 It is written in the Parashat Pinhas, p. 219, that the soul is the companion of the good inclination and the evil inclination because they are angels. And further, it is

written that they are angels that live on high. They have separate intellects. . . . Angels and demons live in the four Foundations and have good and evil inclinations.

On the day of birth, the lower soul enters the infant in this world. Immaturity pervades the infant as it develops under the evil inclination.

. . . The soul is made from the wheels of the World of Making, which is far above the body. The good and evil inclinations raise the body up. It is created from the mass of material from the four Foundations from good and evil. These Foundations are the soul's throne and dress. The soul borrows mass, the body, from below so that it can have life force.

92   The Cause of Causes rides above the four living crea-
      tures of divinity of the World of Emanation. These are
      creatures of strange gods from Samael. There are living
      creatures that climb to the throne of creation. This is
      called intellect.

93   The animal soul in a person lives within the four
      Foundations. It is divided into two parts called the good
      inclination and the evil inclination. They are the throne
      and garment for the soul of a person who might wear
      them on his or her body. Therein lay the secrets of sac-
      rifices of the animal and of the body. This is because the
      animal soul sins. All things that perturb the heart such

as anger, etc., draw harm to the soul. Such things make a soul that desires and covets. It is called the evil inclination.

94   Let us explain the matter of dreams, prophecies, angels and demons. The ten wheels of the World of Making have form and matter. . . . The evil that is in them is called strange gods and idol worship. There are those who worship idols and material things of wheels and stars. . . . There are also those who worship demons.

95   Behold, there is a quiver in the moon that is the lowest wheel. It moves this wheel. It has matter and form. Matter and form are called oppositions of the tail of the quiver. The Lower Ones are near to the Foundation of fire. They hear about the fortunes of the demons that are in the four Foundations. They hear about the wisdoms of the demons that are in the four Foundations and from the wisdom of the raven.

96   Form and soul are likewise in the four Foundations. They are composed of good and evil. From the good were created the children of mankind. They possessed matter and form that originated from the soul of the four Foundations. Demons were created from the evil of the four Foundations. They possessed body and form. Their bodies are composed of the two Foundations of fire and air. They dwell in the secret of the breath of life because

they have a living soul within them. And there are demons that have material souls who dwell in the Earth and in caves. From these demons arise also those who have the souls of plants and they dwell in seas, rivers and pits. These two sorts of demons are called the lower ones. They are very evil. . . . There are also other demons and they are higher than all of the rest. They have a speaking soul and dwell in the Foundation of fire.

97   Angels have matter and form. Their form is very pure. . . . They are heroes. They are pure soul and have divine wisdom whenever they put on their garments. And this is the secret: "And he lifted up his eyes and looked. And lo, three men stood over against him. And when he saw them, he ran to meet them from the tent door, and bowed down to the earth." (Gen. 18:2) This gift is not prophecy, but insight, because he was able to grasp deeply into his intellectual soul and this soul is the soul of that of the angel himself. And thus, those who see Elijah and other higher souls of the righteous every Friday evening, as did our Holy Rabbi, do so only by means of the garment of the robe of the Rabbis.

98   There are ten levels of angels and demons. And although nothing of the angels and demons is created without matter and form, not all of them have garments. All of the heroes, the tenth group, have garments. Angels are separate intellects.

99 Adam is *Ze'ir Anpin*. He had two wives, Leah and Rahel.

100 The Tetragrammaton is composed of simple letters. The majority of the letters are in the image of the feminine and were contained in *Ze'ir Anpin* before the feminine was ever emanated. . . . The feminine is completely strength and judgment. . . . All strengths of the feminine were diffused and hidden inside of *Ze'ir Anpin*.

101 The essence of strength builds the feminine. . . . It went to external worlds to be built up and increase its illuminations and fill *Ze'ir Anpin's* void. . . . The feminine is called *havah*. . . . Flesh is from his flesh . . . .

102 Sefer ha-Tikunin states that Adam had two wives. The first was bone. The second is flesh, weak judgment. Leah was bone, harsh judgment. She was taken from Adam's rib, which is her rightful place. Rahel, however, is flesh because she came from below his chest, from his exposed illuminations. She is called weak judgment. Rahel will be called woman, who is sweetened. Leah is not woman, but she is mixed in shells and is not sweetened. She is Lilith, the mother of the demons. But Leah was sweetened by her prayers and by her tears. . . . Because of her tears and good deeds, her shells were removed. She remained alone, holy and sweetened.

103 Behold, in the beginning, all of the worlds were created in their prescribed order through the strength of *en sof*

and in simple will and grace. Then food, life and emanations had to be given to the worlds so that they might thrive in the World of Creation. It is written: "I know that whatsoever God does, it shall be forever. Nothing can be added to it, nor taken from it. And God made it so that mankind would have fear before Him." (Ecc. 3:14) And further: "That which has been is and is that which shall be. And that which has been done is that which shall be done." (Ecc. 1:9) And it is written: "And on the seventh day God finished the work that he had made. And he rested on the seventh day . . ." (Gen. 2:2) . . . . Created ones are in the image of the higher soul and the external realm. This is because they are mixed among good and evil. Good and evil require good deeds and atonement. . . . Emanations flow faintly to created ones who do not live in atonement. The ten *sefirot* continue to become weaker and fade as they attempt emanate to them. . . .

104 Let us explain the following questions: Why must mankind be created in bodies? Why was mankind made in this way with good and evil inclinations? If these inclinations are evenly balanced within a person, how could free will so incline itself to choose one over the other? And from where does the strength originate that allows a person to do so? And if a person is given the ability to incline toward the good or evil enclinations, should this person be created at all? What is matter? Is mankind's higher soul greater than the angels? And if mankind's

soul is greater than the angels, why did they not descend to this world and dress themselves in bodies and lower souls? . . . How can the King of Kings speak of prophesy—even through an angel!—to lowly mankind?

105 The essence of the worlds consists of *Yod, Hey, Vav, Hey* and are divided into five kinds of spirit worlds: highest soul, sacred soul, life, greater soul, higher emotions and life-force. The material world is the body and matter for these five worlds. All worlds are actually forms of humanity and are composed of matter, form and these five types of spirituality.

106 There is yet another level: ten *sefirot*, divided into 613 images. Every world lives as one world and each part of these worlds is composed of a face of God and they were created from Lower Adam's image.

107 The World of Creation and worlds below it are called the Tree of Knowledge that has both good and evil. As one proceeds downward through these worlds, good decreases and evil increases until the lowest world is reached. Most of the lowest world is evil. The wicked besets the righteous. Law is weak. Right rarely goes forth. If it does go forth, it is perverted. Good is called fruit and evil is called the shell that clothes the fruit. Good lights are the same. The most pure and spiritual within them are

clothed in other lights to the outside. Therefore all lights are arranged according to levels. *En sof* is the innermost of them all. The *sefirot* are ordered within their own levels as well. *Keter* is the innermost. Divine inner presence is the outermost.

108 Behold the fight between matter and the higher soul. The higher soul can only carry out a commandment when it works in unison with the body but the body is more inclined to do evil and it is very difficult to subjugate it. The free will of the higher soul seeks the good inclination but the body must act accordingly in spite of its difficulties to subjugate the evil inclination. Understand this well. When one dies, there is neither punishment for the higher soul nor for the body in separate states. Punishment occurs when they are clothed in each other again, reborn as they were in this life.

109 Israel is *Ze'ir Anpin*. Various branches flow out from *Ze'ir Anpin*. They are Leah, Rahel, Jacob, the Generation of the Wilderness and the Tribes.

110 Rahel is the true *Nukva* of *Ze'ir Anpin*. . . . She is the wife of Israel and she is called *Ze'ir Anpin* at times.

111 The Exterior Ones are called strange gods. They nurse and grasp as they imitate the name of holy Elohim.

112 There is an aspect of the Foundation that reflects immaturity. It is like the snake that bites the womb of the doe. It is the feminine that has not yet matured. . . . Its womb is narrow with severities and judgments until five graces have entered into it.

113 The forepart of female genitalia is the image of the Foundation of divine inner presence of *Nukva*. *Nukva* of *Ze'ir Anpin* is called Rib, People of Israel, Bride of Moses and Upper Rose. *Ze'ir Anpin* is called Moses, Israel and knowledge. Jacob is called *tiferet*. *Nukva* also appears as the rock and lower rose. . . .

114 The Menorah is Rahel. She is the *Nukva* of *Ze'ir Anpin*. She is positioned behind *Ze'ir Anpin*. . . . The lights of *Ze'ir Anpin* are called the lights of the day. The lights of *Nukva* are called the lights of the night.

115 The days of the Exile are 1000 years. . . . The world is to be 6000 years. The first 1000 is with *chessed*, continuing down through these thousands of years until the *yesod*, the sixth 1000. The seventh 1000 is divine inner presence. It is the Sabbath that ascends to God.

116 Leah and Rahel are humility and fear of the Lord.

117 Rahel is called the beginning of wisdom because she is the beginning of all *sefirot* from the lowest to the highest. She is called the woman of valor and fear of the Lord.

118 Leah is called humility because she is behind and above
Ze'ir Anpin. Humility is recognized in a person when that
person lowers his or her head and bends it down opposite
another person, because of this humility and is submis-
sive to that person who is greater.

119 *Ze'ir Anpin* and *Nukva* must return face to face again
through the union of male and female emanations that
are inspired by good deeds and atonement. In this way,
some sparks of the Kings of Edom are purified. The sparks
ascend with the female waters so that little souls might
be created. But *Ze'ir Anpin* and *Nukva* must return to
their previous state again. When they return, they still
live, but remain unconsciousness together, and they do
not have the strength to elevate all of the holy sparks
completely. They have sufficient strength to elevate only
a few at a time.

120 In this our world, we always need purification. But the
Kings of Edom were pure from the beginning. . . . If
Adam had not sinned, there would have been atonement
and therefore there would be no need for this lower world.
The purpose of this world is to purify. Adam ate from the
Tree of Knowledge that is mixed with good with evil. He
sinned in the upper mating that was intended to occur
after sundown on Friday. Good would then have been
separated from evil. The good in the upper world would
have been purified and the evil would have descended

below. Because of his sin, they remained mixed and holy sparks fell into the shells.

121 Adam saw that the snake was mating with Havah and he desired to do that act. Adam was created during daylight on Friday, the eve of the Sabbath. If he would have waited to mate until Friday evening . . . the mating would have been proper and all of Adam's semen would have been without evil. But since Adam chose to mate during the day, filth mixed with his semen. This signifies the Tree of Knowledge, good and evil. The snake put its filth into the daylight hours through Friday until sunset because the shells gather during this time. The shells want to receive the same holy illumination so that they might have life during the forthcoming week. This is why it is written that one must wash the hands and the feet on the eve of the Sabbath.

122 Our Rabbis of blessed memory said that Abel looked at the *Shekhinah* and merited death. Cain killed him for this reason. Had it been for any other reason, the Holy One, Blessed Be He, would have guarded him. The reason is: "And when the woman saw the tree was good for food, and that it was a delight to the eyes, and that the tree was to be desired to make one wise, she took of the fruit thereof, and did eat. And she also gave it unto her husband with her. And he did eat." (Gen. 3:6) It is, because

she sinned by looking at the Tree and also caused her son to sin by looking with his eyes.

123 The lowest of the seven Heavens is called Vilon [curtain] and it is of no service at all except that evening leaves and the morning enters.

124 Heaven has sun, moon and constellations set in it. These are located in the Foundation of Tevunah. Heaven is the small Hebrew letter *Vav*. It is hidden in the secret: "He who stretches out the heavens like a curtain." (Ps. 104:2)

125 The sun and the moon have been put in the heavens and lights come from them.

The sun and the moon are *Ze'ir Anpin*.

126 Rahel's *keter* begins just beneath the heels of Leah. Our Rabbis have said that fear forged the crown for her head and humility made the heel of her sole. The legs of Leah (humility) forged fear (Rahel) called the *keter* for her head.

127 Adam's sin caused darkness in *Abba*. *Abba* is not recognizable in creation. Only *Ima* is recognizable there. This is the secret: *Ima* builds in the creation within the three

upper *sefirot* of the thrones. . . ." He made darkness his hiding place, his pavilion round about him. Darkness of waters, thick clouds of the skies." (Ps. 18:12) And *Abba* and *Ima* are in the creation of impurity and they issue reparation to those below them. The light continues to the impure ones from *Abba* and *Ima*.

128 The body of *Ze'ir Anpin* of the World of Creation is called Metataron. The Body of *Nukva* of *Ze'ir Anpin* is called Sandalfon.

129 *Nefesh* from *rakia vilon* first enters into a person. . . . The person is given only a lower soul from the World of Making. Then follows the holy intellectual part of the lower soul. . . . Then a person draws higher emotions and soul from the World of Formation. . . .

The soul increases to its highest level called *neshamah*. . . . The person binds all the worlds from inside and from outside. How? Behold in the World of Making, a person is given a body from the Earth. . . . And inside of the person is the basic soul in the image of shells. But deeper within a person are reflections of angels. The angels within were created for all of the needs of the worlds.

130 And when a person is deficient in observing some commandment, that special limb, which is related to the commandment, will lack food. And that limb will ultimately die. When the holiness departs from it, then the spirit of impurity in it will be dressed from the four Foundations of the lower soul of impurity. And the limb is then fed impure bread.

131 And when a person sins, a branch must be cut from the person, as from the branch of a tree. It then remains separated from it and stands in this world like the spirit of an animal.

132 And behold, the holy one, blessed be he, gave the Torah and commandments to Israel to purify and to remove drosses from the silver that clothes the higher soul. The covering of the higher soul carries out good intentions and deeds for mankind according to the Torah and the commandments.

Benedictions of the Soul

Repair of the Worlds

1   Adam's body was made from the World of Creation. He was hewn from the Throne of Glory.

2   It spanned itself majestically through every world, from the first to the very last of countless worlds. Adam was all worlds of the 6000 years of the existence of mankind.

3   Adam lived in the highest of all realms. . . . He was higher than all of the angels, higher than the Metataron.

4   All worlds lived in tremendous glory . . . they stood infinitely high above the depths. But they fell into these depths after the sin of Adam.

5   The highest and most blessed souls lived in Adam.

6   The souls in Adam are allotted many years of existence so that they can enter into lower souls and help their worlds continue existence. Through proper meditations and works, lower souls might then be made whole again.

7   The Divine One gave worlds and souls 6000 years of existence so that the higher souls from all worlds would be made whole again in unity with It.

8   The higher souls will exist for 6000 years for this special purpose.

9   There will be 2000 years of *tohu*, 2000 years of Torah, 2000 years of days of the Messiah.

10   The Kings of Edom possessed excessive severity when our world was created. They lay among the wreckage of shells in the worlds, deeply imbued in matter and external powers. Their souls must rise within female waters above these powers, that is, above the Worlds of Creation, Formation and Making.

11   The seven kings . . . are the image of the face of Adam, from his head to his feet, now sunk into matter. Upper mating makes sparks from Adam ascend in holiness in the secret of female waters. They join with male waters. From these waters highest souls were born.

12   Female waters are holy souls. They are in the Kings of Edom. The kings must be purified as they lay in their lowly state so that they can ascend in the image of these waters. Male waters will join with them by way of mating of male and of female. From these two aspects highest souls are created.

13   All worlds moved higher, joined into one world, and lived inside of the World of Emanation. They were completely holy. They remained in the emanated world as the Worlds of Creation, Formation and Making, comprised of thirty *sefirot* in pure and open space.

14   Then Adam also ascended so that his entire body was in the Garden of Eden, which is *Nukva* of the World of Emanation.

15   If Adam had not sinned in the Tree of Knowledge, he would have been able to make the worlds ascend even higher through his prayers.

16   The World of Emanation, with all worlds in great unity, would have ascended to their first place, to the palace of Adam Kadmon, to the place where all existence first begins.

17   All worlds were about to return existence to its first root, to its cause of causes.

18 All worlds have two aspects: exterior and interior. You must know that the worlds indeed ascended with both of these remarkable qualities.

19 But they fell because of the sin of Adam.

20 Adam caused all of the exiles that have been and are to be, until the days of the Messiah come.

21 There were only four exiles after Israel was exiled and scattered among seventy nations: Babylon, Medea, Greece and Edom.

22 In the shells are four rivers, two of which are Pishon (Kingdom of Babylon) and Gihon (Kingdom of Medea). These are the roots. And they are divided into seventy nations. The seventy nations are part of these four rivers. Israel was exiled from every nation of these four.

23 The remaining seventy nations comprise the branches of these four rivers. Higher souls fell among these nations.

24 Israel must go to the nations into which higher souls fell. Their exile is necessary so that they might be able to purify the sparks and save those higher souls that fell among the nations.

25 The Exile of Egypt preceded all of the exiles.

26   In the beginning the *Shekhinah* descended and clothed herself in the shells and she is called the head. Her presence is active throughout the body.

27   In the exiles of Egypt and Babylon, Israel was exiled in Egypt as the head. . . . It was written that Israel's ". . . head was of gold. . . ." (Dan. 2:32)

28   But in the Exile of Greece and Edom, all ten tribes were not exiled . . . and they are not part of the head, which is Israel.

29   The sparks of the two-and-a-half tribes that were exiled among them were scattered and mixed.

30   Great souls come from upper mating, from emanations, from drops of graces and severities that exist in higher knowledge. (Gen. 4:1: And Adam knew Eve his wife . . .)

31   Higher mating is the language of knowing.

32   Its emanation springs forth from divine inner consciousness of higher knowledge.

33   The seeds of . . . divine consciousness of grace and severity are reserved for the births of off-springs, just as grace and severity might be seen in a son or in a daughter.

34   Graces and severities build the body of a newborn child.

35 Our scholars of blessed memory once said that the
    righteous descend to Gehinom, to a dwelling place in
    the shells, after they die. The righteous grasp onto the
    wicked and save them while they live among the shells.

36 Oh! Hear the secret! It is in this way that the righteous
    cause upper mating between *Zeir* and *Nukva* at the time
    of their death.

37 And also hear! The death of the righteous is by a kiss.
    (*Talmud*, Baba Bathra, 17a)

38 Our Rabbis taught "There were six over whom the Angel
    of Death had no dominion. But they died by a divine
    kiss—Abraham, Isaac and Jacob, Moses, Aaron and Miram.
    Moses, Aaron and Miriam died in this way, because they
    died by the mouth of the Lord. (Num. 33:38)

39 The secret is written in the *Zohar* Va-yakhel 211a: When
    a lower righteous one dies, I will clothe the upper righ-
    teous in envy. And the lower righteous one will join
    with *Nukva* in divine consciousness. The righteous one's
    soul purifies the higher souls that were in Gehinom, the
    dwelling place of the shells. They raise these souls up in
    the mystery of female waters and arouse more upper mat-
    ing. Higher souls are made whole again in this way.

40 Not everyone who wishes to say the Tetragramaton can
    do so because he or she might not be able to grasp it

fully and with true intention. But whoever is completely righteous and worthy through good merits can descend to purify sparks inside the shells even if they resist. A person must take care to complete each prayer in devout intention from its beginning to its end. If a person does not do this, then when he or she transfers the soul to descend among the shells, it will not be able to purify the souls that have fallen there. And further, that person's life force and lower soul will be trapped inside of the shells.

41 Similarly, if a righteous person dies in this world, that person will be able to descend into the shells and make the souls ascend that had fallen into this clinging mud of Gehinom in the secret of the shells. And whoever has lesser ability to ascend will still be able to escape the shells, but must do so alone, without being able to save others who are trapped there. A wicked person who descends to Gehinom remains in Gehinom.

42 This is prostration. A complete and righteous person can descend among the shells to purify, free and ascend with the souls that fell according to the secret of female waters. But the person who isn't strong enough to purify, free and ascend with these souls, can still escape and ascend from there upon his or her own power. But a person's soul could remain among the shells after having descended there during prostration and that person would have no hope of escape.

43   When one sleeps, one is within the secret of death, because the soul descends to the Tree of Death among the shells. And there are others who can then purify, gather and ascend with souls in female waters in order to join in the language of knowing at night.

44   We also discovered an astonishing thing. A completely righteous person [who descends among the shells] might change into someone entirely different, even into a wicked person. This was the case for Yohanan, the high priest who served eighty years in the priesthood. He was made a Sadducee. Whenever a person's soul goes down to death among the shells during prostration, he or she might still be in sin and the soul might not be able to ascend above the shells again. The shells grasp it and it remains there forever. The shells then replace this soul with a wicked one that came from the shells. And this is what our Rabbis of blessed memory have said: "But the dead know nothing." These are the wicked that in their lifetime are called dead.

45   And therefore, behold, I am warning you very much in this matter: A person should take great care in true intention with regard to prostration. The person must be completely righteous. If the person is not completely righteous, then he or she must be profoundly intent in the utterance of the prayer from its beginning and until its very end.

46 Whoever completes prostration in the way that I have described experiences no end to the rewards that unfold for doing it. Whoever completes such prostration causes the upper union of the language of knowing, purifies the worlds below, and pours wholeness into the purifications that exist inside of the shells.

47 Whosoever completes prostration in good intention sees his enemies fall before him after his prayers . . . (*Talmud*, Baba Mezia, 59b A Tanna taught: Great was the calamity that befell that day, for everything upon which R. Eliezer cast his eyes was burned up.)

48 In prostration, one falls upon one's face. Behold, because when we fall on our faces, we are in the prayer of Eighteen Benedictions, standing in the World of Emanation. And while in the World of Emanation, we are also in *Nukva* of *Ze'ir Anpin* of Rahel. We are her servants, her sons and daughters who make to ascend female waters to her for her sake. And we make ourselves fall from above, from the World of Emanation, where we are now in this state of prayer. And we descend below until we find ourselves at the end of the World of Making. We do this as a person who might throw him or herself from the top of a roof to the ground below. And this is the true secret of the intention of prostration.

49 And when, within heartfelt righteous intention, we have thrown ourselves to the end of the World of Making,

we gather and purify female waters from there. Next, we visualize that we ascend from the World of Making to the World of Formation to likewise gather and to purify female waters from there. From there, we intend to ascend to the World of Creation to gather and to purify from there. And from there we ascend to the World of Emanation and enter again into *Nukva* of *Ze'ir Anpin*. Then we make the purified female waters that we have gathered flow inside of her foundation within this mystery.

50   Remember that these purified sparks are not able to ascend by themselves. A person must intend to participate with his or her own soul in order to rescue them. These purifications will be able to ascend with a person's lower, higher, and highest soul. The sparks are purified while still trapped in the shells themselves.

51   Finally, we intend to make our souls descend to the World of Making. They will then gather and purify from this world those purifications that we find and we will make them rise with us. These great actions occur in the power of the merit of the commandment of prayer, which we keep within.

52   Prostration is discussed in the *Zohar* Va-yakhel 200b. It says that while a person is in prostration, that person deposits his or her soul in the Tree of Death and goes down to death. It is said that the person is in the great

wilderness. The true aspect of death resides in the shells, according to the mystery: "Her feet go down to death" (Prov. 5:5). A person must go down to death, truly strive to lower his or her soul to this place among the shells, and then, with fullest intention to remove it again, to return from death through goodness and merits of prayer and purifications, that occur in the place of death. This happens by way of the lower soul, the life force, which originates in the World of Making. The person will gather these purifications from there and join with them. Then they ascend from the World of Making to the World of Formation. And there, by means of the person's higher soul that originates from this higher World of Formation, the person strives to likewise make purifications that are in the World of Formation and make them ascend from there to the World of Creation. And there, by means of his highest soul, which is from the World of Creation, the person strives in good faith to make purifications that are likewise necessary in the World of Creation. Then the person will make the purifications from all of these three worlds ascend until the highest World of Emanation. The person then experiences the soul's totality in full-ness of heart (life force, higher and highest levels) as it participates in the three states of purifications. He or she will then allow the purifications to enter inside of the Foundation of the *Nukva* of *Ze'ir Anpin* of the World of Emanation. And then, male waters will descend from the male's Foundation. And then, the emanation and great light that reside in male waters will descend to the soul's life force, higher and highest levels of this person. Such is the person who makes the prostration and causes this great commandment. And a great light will be emanated in this person that is so pure that it will truly be worthy of the soul's profoundest being, because without a doubt, whoever completes this great commandment by going down to death to the three worlds in order to purify souls and to cause *Zeir* and *Nukva* to join in divine consciousness, will have immeasurable reward. And therefore that drop of male water will finally descend so that it will be mixed with those purified states (female waters) and they will be purified in fullness and be able to create new and good creations.

53   The upper male waters descend for the person who makes prostration. The light thickens in the person's lower soul and as it enters there it becomes renewed, whole and complete. This mystery is expressed in *Zohar* Va-yakhel 200b, which says that a person who intends prostration takes a share in the blessings of all blessings, because this person causes so much good among the worlds. And the person experiences so much completeness that comes from the firmament that he or she actually becomes an aspect of the Foundation itself, which is called *shalom*.

54   In the time of the destruction of the temple and sin, shells increased. The ten martyrs transferred their bodies to active divine presence below. They became female waters for human existence. They let their souls, the

sparks that were trapped in shells, ascend to the female waters of *Abba* and *Ima*.

55   Know the secret: "Flee then from the Land of the North, says the Lord. For I have spread you abroad as the four winds of heaven, says the Lord." (Zech. 2:10) Israel must go into exile, into all the four winds of heaven and in all of the seventy nations.

56   Those higher souls do not have the strength to escape the shells, unless they are freed by means of the commandments and by the prayers of Israel. They can purify themselves while within these shells, rise above them and ascend within the female waters.

57   The righteous do not enter the dwelling place of shells to be punished. On the contrary, they assuage the Gehinom for goodness so that it is can not rule over them. They go there to pluck the higher souls that are dispersed among the shells in the Gehinom. And they make them ascend from the shells with them. Then they enter into the secret female waters and all enjoy wholeness together among the male waters. And then, they come into this world in the bodies of the lower ones as the remaining blessed souls of Israel. The righteous complete this work during their life and death so that they might continue to purify the higher souls and to help them ascend above the shells and to free the nations from exile.

58 The wicked are dead during their lifetimes because their higher souls refuse to live in them. Their higher souls flee into the living Elohim because of their sins. These higher souls escape through the Foundations of the wicked. Lower souls come from shells and they replace higher souls that had left and entered into the wicked. They are therefore called the living dead. The desire of shells strives toward evil and seeks to overtake human beings so that they might sin and give them the upper hand in order to grasp into holy souls and into life itself. They feed from holy souls and receive life from them. Holy souls in shells are as holy souls in the body. The souls give the body life. Shells pursue all exterior ones and cling wherever there is holiness because they cling there to live; if they stop clinging, they die. Do not be surprised how voraciously these shells pursue human beings in order to make their children sin and to raise their Creator to anger. They do this selfishly and with no regard toward holiness.

59 Understand why the wicked are punished for their sins and how fitting it is for them to be punished. They desecrate holiness, embrace profanity and give the shells life.

60 When we confess, graces descend to our hearts. We say:

Amighty King, who sits upon the throne of mercy, you act graciously and pardon the sins of thy people and make them pass away one by one. You often grant pardon to sinners; you forgive transgressors; you deal generously with all mortals and you do not respond to the measure of wickedness that they truly deserve. O God, you instructed us to recite the thirteen divine qualities, remember, for our favor, the covenant of the thirteen qualities, as you revealed them to gentle Moses, as it is written: "The lord came down in the cloud, and Moses placed himself there beside him and proclaimed the name of the Lord. Then the Lord passed by before him, and proclaimed: 'The Lord, the lord is a merciful and gracious God, slow to anger and abounding in kindness and truth; he keeps mercy for thousands of generations, forgiving iniquity and transgression and sin and forgiving those who repent.'" O pardon our iniquity and sin, and make us thy very own. Our Father, forgive us, for we have sinned; our King, pardon us, for we have transgressed. Thou, O Lord, art truly kind, forgiving and merciful to all who call upon thee.

And this causes union of emanations with Leah from the breast and above because graces already descended there. It is there that the heart is revealed. And now, in prostration, the graces descend to the Foundation of *Ze'ir Anpin* . . . and they descend and join in unity with Rahel in the secret of emanations.

Behold this matter of prostration. Now is the time for the drop of male waters of graces to descend in emanations of unity to join with *Nukva*. . . . The flow of female waters must precede these events so that they might accept the male waters and be in union with these emanations, according to the secret that if a woman emits seed first, the child will be a boy; if the man first emits seed, the child will be a girl. Female waters arise in emanation when they are purified and cleansed by our prayers each day. They are cleansed of the seven kings who died. When they are purified of these dregs, the female waters ascend.

We will now think of prostration of the morning prayer. Yisrael and Leah joined in emanation through the prayer of the Thirteen Attributes:

"The Lord"

"The Lord"

"God"

"Merciful"

"Gracious"

"Long-suffering"

"Abundant in goodness and truth"

"Keeping mercy unto the thousandth generation"

"Forgiving iniquity"

"Forgiving transgression"

"Forgiving sin"

"Remembering the guilty"

"Visiting iniquity of the fathers upon the children until the third and fourth generations."

And now, with the prostration, Jacob and Lea join in emanation.

When we confess, we profess the thirteen attributes, we confess as we do in the prayer, Sim Shalom:

O grant peace, happiness, blessing, grace, kindness and mercy to us and to all Israel thy people. Bless us all alike, our Father, with the light of thy countenance; indeed, by the light of thy countenance thou hast given us, Lord our God, a Torah of life, loving-kindness, charity, blessing, mercy, life and peace. May it please thee to bless thy people Israel with peace at all times and hours.

May all Israel, thy people, be remembered and inscribed before thee in the book of life and blessing, peace and prosperity, for a happy life and for peace. Blessed art thou, O Lord, Author of peace.

Our God and God of our fathers, may our prayer reach thee; do not ignore our plea. We can never to be so insolent nor so obstinate as to say to Lord our God and God of our fathers: "We are just and have not sinned."

Indeed, we have sinned.

We have acted treasonably, aggressively and slanderously;
We have acted brazenly, viciously and fraudulently;

We have acted willfully, scornfully and obstinately;
We have acted perniciously, disdainfully and erratically.

Turning away from thy good precepts and laws has not profited us. Thou art just in all that has come upon us; thou hast dealt truthfully, but we have acted wickedly. O thou who dwellest on high, what can we say to thee? Thou knowest the mysteries of the universe and the dark secrets of every living soul. Thou dost search all the inmost chambers of man's conscience; nothing escapes thee. Nothing is hidden from thy sight. Now, may it be thy will, Lord our God, and God of our fathers, to forgive all of our sins, to pardon all of our iniquities, and to grant atonement for all of our transgressions. For we have committed the sins thus:

1. In thy sight forcibly or willingly;
2. Against thee by idle talk;
3. In thy sight unintentionally;
4. Against thee by idle talk;
5. In thy sight by lustful behavior;
6. Against thee publicly or privately;
7. Against thee by offensive speech;
8. In thy sight by oppressing a fellow person;
9. Against thee by evil thoughts;
10. In thy sight by lewd association;
11. Against thee by insincere confession;
12. By contempt for parents or teachers;

13. Against thee willfully or by mistake;
14. In thy sight by violence;
15. Against thee by defaming the name;
16. In thy sight by unclean lips;
17. Against thee by foolish talk;
18. In thy sight by the evil impulse;
19. Against thee wittingly or unwittingly.

Forgive us all sins, O God of forgiveness and grant us atonement for sinning thus:

20. In thy sight by fraud and falsehood;
21. Against thee by bribery;
22. In thy sight by scoffing;
23. Against thee by slander;
24. In thy sight in dealings with people;
25. Against thee in eating and drinking and in thy sight by usury and interest;
26. Against thee by a lofty bearing;
27. In thy sight by our manner of speech;
28. Against thee by wanton glances;
29. In thy sight by haughty airs;
30. Against thee by scornful defiance.

Forgive us all our sins. For sinning thus:

31. In thy sight by casting off responsibility;
32. Against thee in passing judgment;
33. In thy sight by plotting against people;

33. Against thee by sordid selflessness;
34. In thy sight by levity of mind;
35. Against thee by being obstinate;
36. In thy sight by running to do evil;
37. Against thee by telling untruths;
38. In thy sight by swearing falsely;
39. Against thee by groundless hatred;
40. In thy sight by breach of trust;
41. Against thee by a confused heart.

Forgive us all our sins. For the sins that require:

1. a burnt offering;
2. a sin offering;
3. varying offerings;
4. guilt offerings;
5. corporeal punishment;
6. forty lashes;
7. premature death;
8. requiring excision and childlessness.

Forgive us the sins for which the early courts would inflict death penalties by stoning, burning, beheading or strangling; forgive us the breach of positive commands and the breach of negative commands, whether or not they involve an act, whether or not they are known to us. The sins already known to us we have already acknowledged to thee; and those that are not known to us are indeed well known to thee, as it is said: What is hidden belongs to the Lord our God, but what is known concerns us and our children forever, that we may observe all the commands of this Torah. Thou art the forgiver of Israel. . . . Without you we have no King to pardon and forgive our sins.

My God, before I was formed I was of no worth, and now that I have been formed it is as if I have not been formed. Dust I am in life, and all the more so in death. In thy sight, I am like an object filled with shame and disgrace. May it be thy will, Lord my God and God of my fathers, that I sin no more. In thy abundant mercy, cleanse the sins that I have committed against thee, but not through severe sufferings.

61 "Nevertheless you shall die like men. And fall like one of the princes." (Ps. 82:7) and: "But as for you, your carcasses shall fall in this Wilderness." (Num. 14:32) The first pure body is the garment that is clothed in the Garden of Eden of the Earth. Subsequently, death follows. The filth of the Animal Body of Evil is contained in the four Foundations. It is written: "And they will go forth. And look upon the carcasses of the men that have rebelled against Me." (Is. 66:24) For their worm shall not die. Neither shall their fire be quenched. And they shall be an abhorring unto all flesh. This is the form that is the evil. It is in the animal soul.

62   This foul body is the world. It is made from all of the worlds. The waste of these worlds forms their matter. The heavens and the souls within them are the angels of good and evil who live in the glowing shells. Even they are made from matter. Adam's body is of matter. The power if inner brightness and glowing shells of good and evil are in Adam.

63   The true body is glowing shells. It is the garment for the life force, higher emotions and the highest soul. After Adam's sin, glowing shells mixed among good and evil changed. They must be purified by means of the Torah and the commandments. This will occupy Israel until the coming of the Messiah.

64   Consider the secret of prostration. When the priests and the people who stood in the court heard the glorious and awful name pronounced out of the mouth of the high priest, in holiness and in purity, they knelt and prostrated themselves and made acknowledgment. They fell upon their faces and praised his blessed, glorious and sovereign name.

65   The words of our Rabbis, of blessed memory, are well known. They have described the great extent of the many troubles that will be in store for Israel as it endures the birth pangs of the Messiah. These are for completion of the purification of holiness. Imperfection and pain are in the feet of Adam among the shells. The exterior ones grow stronger while holiness grows weaker. When the feet and legs of Adam among the shells become whole and are purified, it is written: "He will swallow up death forever. And the Lord God will wipe away tears off all faces. And he will take away the reproach of his people from off all of the earth. For the Lord has spoken it." (Is. 28:7)

66   The Exile of Egypt is remembered more than all the rest of the Exiles. This is because the sparks of the Head of Israel were mixed throughout Egypt. These sparks were not redeemed nor rescued from Egypt until their purification throughout the soul's highest levels.

67   The people of Israel are as fish. . . . The people of Israel are as grain.

68   So shall they fear the name of the Lord from the west. And so shall they praise his glory from the rising of the sun. Distress will come in like a flood, driven by the breath of the Lord. It has been said by our Rabbis, of blessed memory, Israel will have great troubles and gather strength in its birth pains of the Messiah. This is because Israel will enter the end of the age of purifications as Adam's legs are among matter and evil. Isreal will feel exterior ones grow stronger as holiness grows weaker and begins to fade away. And when Adam's

legs have completed purification, it is written: "Bila ha-mavet la-netsah." (Is. 25:8, He will swallow up death for ever. . . .)

69   Matter still rules over holiness; its emanations fade and vanish.

70   While Israel lives under subjugation, the tail rules. They are shells and have authority over holiness. And great emanations are drawn to this holiness. From this holiness, Israel's share flows to the rest of the nations.

71   Israel will be the lowliest of the kingdoms and it will not lift itself up above the nations. Powerful kingdoms will be diminished and they shall no longer rule over the nations. Israel still exists. The essence of the shells of the seventy nations still exists. The souls of holiness are inside of them. They give Egypt, Babylon, Media and Greece a part of their emanations.

72   In the time to come all holiness will be purified from inside of each of the seventy Officers and their life will depart from them. Shells shall no longer grasp and nurse. Then, these shells, complete death, will be done away with.

73   There will be no exile forever.

74   In the future to come all Holiness will be purified from inside of all the seventy Officers and their life will depart.

There will no longer be grasping, nursing nor life to gen-erate such suffering within. Then *kelipot*, will be entirely abrogated. It is written: He will swallow up death for ever. (Is. 25:8) And all exiles will be swallowed up forever.

75   Divine inner presence is the last *Hey* in the Tetra-grammaton. It is the kingdom, the female, the mem-brane, *Hey*. Because of this membrane, the feminine, the *Hey*, is formed.

76   In the time of destruction and sin, shells increased. This is the secret of the ten martyrs. . . . They transferred their bodies to divine inner presence and became *mayin nukvin* for the kingdom. They let their souls, the sparks that were trapped in shells, ascend to the *mayin nukvin* of *Abba* and *Ima*.

77   Adam's sleep at night is close to the secret of death. His soul makes great descents to the Tree of Death in the place of the shells. And then, one purifies and gathers the souls. They ascend according to the mysteries of *mayin nukvin* and mate at night . . . Some souls remain alone in the *kelipot* and do not ascend at all.

78   Israel must continue in exile below and exist in every nation to gather roses of the sacred highest souls, which dispersed inside the thorns.

79   Adam's sin mixed good with evil. And all the blessed highest souls fell into the shells . . . the shells are the seventy nations. And Israel must be in Exile among all of them, in order to gather the blessed ones that fell inside the *kelipah*. Israel is in them.

80   In the time to come, *Ze'ir Anpin* and *Nukva* will be forever complete. There will no longer be deceit and transgression in the world. . . . *Ze'ir Anpin* will be illuminated in wholeness and have his own full soul. He will be a countenance of ten complete *sefirot*. He will be equal to his highest self, *Abba*. . . . In this present world *Ze'ir Anpin* is imperfect and weak, although not always. . . . He is composed of only his six *sefirot*. He can not mate in emanations with his *Nukva* and be united with it in perfect unity. But in the time to come *Ze'ir Anpin* will be equal in the value of his *Abba*. *Ze'ir Anpin* will be one and his *Nukva* will be one. They will be united in one eternal union like *Abba* and *Ima*, who are always in one union and whose mating does not stop forever.

81   And therefore the female that is death and the male that is the shadow of death [mentioned in Parashat Pekude] will generate life forever.

82   . . . The Earth is the active divine presence. The heavens are *Ze'ir Anpin*.

83   The purpose of the development of all of these worlds is to make whole again and to purify. Purification is possible only by distancing the holy from the less holy in a gradual fashion and to further develop that which is less holy.

84   The vessels died and descended to the World of Creation. Waste remained there. And in the time of the *tikkun* spiritual food was again made pure and ascended above in emanation. The exterior ones and matter rule only within *Zeir* and *Nukva* and they are called the seven days of creation, in which the world was created. The world will be built with love and grace.

85   We are with the world, we are all Israel, created by *Zeir* and *Nukva*. We are their children.

Notes

[1] Moshe Idel rightly points out that "The expulsion of the Jews from the Iberian Peninsula was seen as structuring Lurianic Kaballa's particular interest in the questions of exile, messianism and evil. . . . Lurianic texts never mention the expulsion . . . I only suggest that, given the absence of Lurianic discussion of the expulsion issue, Scholem's universally accepted theory regarding the interconnection of the two is in fact only one of many options that could easily be advanced; the demonstration of their validity, of course, would be difficult if not impossible." Moshe Idel, *Kabbalah: New Perspectives* (New Haven: Yale University Press, 1990), p. 265.

[2] Hayyim Vital, 1542 *Book of Visions*, trans. Morris M. Faierstein in *Jewish Mystical Autobiographies* (New Jersey: Paulist Press, 1999), p. 156.

[3] See Joseph Dan, "Ethics in Sixteenth-Century Safed," *Jewish Mysticism and Jewish Ethics* (Seattle: University of Washington Press, 1986), pp. 92–127.

[4] See Yehuda Liebes in "Myth vs. Symbol in the Zohar and in Lurianic Kaballah," *Essential Papers on Kabbalah*, ed. by Lawerence Fine (New York: New York University Press, 1995), pp. 225–227.

[5] Luria's gravid symbolism reflects not only imperfection (see note 14) but also death and regeneration as aspects of the divine, imbedded in the essence of all spirituality. "After the return of the line of light of *En sof* which was to be inside of the vessels, the light of Adam Kadmon's essence, his bones, returned and was contained inside of the vessels. The light remained as vessels and as the impression of his essence, his bones."*Hekhal* 1. Adam kadmon. *Shaar* (Gate) 1. *Derush agulim ve-yosher. Anaf* 1., p. 25. See also: Adam kadmon. Vital, Hayyim ben Joseph, 1542 or 3–1620. *Peri ets hayim.* (Tel Aviv: *Hotsa'at Kitve Rabenu ha-Ari*, 726–[1965 or 1966], v. 5.) *Mavo shearim. Shaar* 1. *Helek* 1., p. 3. See also David Biale "Sixteenth Century Jewish Mysticism" in *An Introduction to Medieval Mystics in Europe*, ed. Paul Szarmach (New York: SUNY Press, 1984), p. 323.

[6] Dan, "Ethics in Sixteenth-Century Safed," pp. 98–100.

[7] C.G. Jung, *Wandlungen und Symbole der Libido* (München: Deutscher Taschenbuch Verlag, 1990), p. 44.

[8] Liebes, "Myth vs. Symbol in the Zohar and in Lurianic Kaballah, p. 226. See also Eliahu Klein's book, *Kabbalah of Creation* (New Jersey: Jason Aronson, Inc., 2000). Rabbi Klein stresses that the significance of Luria's work lies in his spiritual teachings and its potential power to transform each human being. See his Introduction, p. 5.

[9] Hayyim ben Joseph Vital (1542), *Peri 'ets hayim*, (Tel Aviv: Hotsa'at Kitve Rabenu ha-Ari, 726–[1965]), *Hekhal* I, *Shaar* I, Article 2, p. 25.

[10] Vital, *Peri 'ets hayim*, Branch 2, Chapter 1, Article 2, p. 28.

[11] ". . . the spread of light and its subsequent disappearance cause the existence of a vessel." Luria illustrates this transcendental pulse by comparing it to a candle, as has been shown in the Zohar. This pulse is like the flickering of a candle. It arrives and does not arrive. The ontology of vessels and of the continued existence of all *sefiroth* are made possible through emanation and the *withdrawal* of its light. The full description of the ontology and its dynamic is not only interesting but quite complex and beyond the scope of this paper. See Vital, *Peri 'ets hayim*, Shaar 7, *Perek 1 Mati ve-lo mati*, pp. 92–93.

[12] Klein, *Kabbalah of Creation*, pp. 138–140.

[13] The dynamic of Lurianic ontology can best be summed up in Scholem's *über einige Grundbegriffe des Judentums* (Frankfurt am Main: Suhrkamp, 1970), Ch 2. Nothing in Luria's cosmogony is

static. Everything exists in the organic flux of divine synergy. I translate from pages 86–87:

"God sent a beam of his light into the *tehiru*, which was created through the act of *tsimtsum*. Hence the creation is emanation upon every level, but it is at the same time a renewed and continual drawing together and withdrawal of the Divine One. Because if the *tsimtsum*—that limitation of God into himself—were not continual, God would just be alone. All non-divine existence would *eo ipso* disappear when the *tsimtsum* ceases. Therefore a deep dialectic is given within every being that is created according to the *tsimtsum*: The nothingness of *tsimtsum* penetrates into all being pervasively. There is no pure being and no pure nonbeing. Everything that exists results from the double motion in which God takes into himself and yet, at the same time, emanates back. Both processes are mutually unresolvable and limiting. The process of emanation that shares something of the divine with all beings in every point, on each level, is limited by God's continual return to himself. The divine progression expresses itself through the lowest level of all that exists in a continually renewed moment of moving into itself and of moving out of itself. . . . The nothingness of God's essence that remains because he has withdrawn himself may be viewed as residue, as the impression from the previous state of being."

[14] See Vital, *Peri 'ets hayim, Hekhal* 1. Adam kadmon. *Shaar.* (Gate) 5. *Teamim, Nekudim, Tagim, Otiyot. Perek* 6., p. 73. Moreover, there was a split in the navel of Adam Kadmon. This symbol of imperfection points to previous worlds that failed and now seek to right themselves through divine regeneration that is reflected in our present creation. This imperfection influenced the death of the Kings of Edom and, of course, all pre-creation. *Hekhal* I, Ch 6, *Perek* 5, p. 84. See also Yechiel Bar-Lev in *Song of the Soul* (New York: Dagush International, 1994), pp. 152–154.

[15] Rainer Maria Rilke, *The Selected Poetry of Rainer Maria Rilke*, ed. by Stephen Mitchel (London: Pan Books, 1982), Duino Elegy # 7, p. 191. trans. author of this article.

[16] "*Est unum quod nunquam moritur, quoniam augmentatione perpetua perseverat; cum corpus glorificatum fuerit in resurrectione novissima mortuorum. . . Tunc Adam secundus dicet priori et filiis suis: Venite benedicti patris mei.*" Marie-Louise von Franz, *Aurora Consurgens* (document attributed to Thomas Aquinas), in C. G. Jung, *Mysterium Coniunctionis*, 14/III (Zürich: Walter Olten, 1957), trans. C. G. Jung. Available in English: *Aurora Consurgens* (Toronto: Inner City Books, 2000). First published in 1966 as a companion volume to C. G. Jung's *Mysterium Coniunctionis*, her work bears out Jung's long-standing view that alchemy is best understood symbolically, as an attempt to express unconscious psychic images through their projection onto matter.

[17] "The myth of the shattered vessels and their ultimate restoration (*tikkun*) was for the Ari not merely a theory about distant times and transcendent worlds, but something very much alive, revealed in the faces of those around him." See Yehuda Liebes in "Myth vs. Symbol in the Zohar and in Lurianic Kaballah," p. 227. Malaise of the soul and the visages that adhere to it are well illustrated as archetypes of the subconscious in C. G. Jung's *Archetypen* (München: Deutscher Taschenbuch Verlag, 1993). See also *Die Archetypen und das kollektive Unbewußte*, v. 9/I *Gesammelte Werke* (Olten, 1971–1990).

[18] Scholem, *Von der Mystischen Gestalt der Gottheit*, p. 32.

[19] "To the Ari, souls are the inner essence of higher worlds." This fits his belief in the transmigration of souls. See Liebes, "Myth vs. Symbol in the Zohar and in Lurianic Kaballah," p. 226.

[20] See Vital, *Peri 'ets hayim Hekhal* VII, Gates 43 and 47, pp. 319–322, p. 367; *Hekhal* VI, Gate 35, *perek* 1, p. 166. For detailed discussions of sefiroth see Bar-Lev in *Song of the Soul*, pp. 71–111 and Moses Luzzatto *General Principles of the Kabbalah*, trans. The Research Centre of Kabbalah (New York: Weiser, 1970), pp. 1–12.

[21] See Vital, *Peri 'ets hayim, Shaar* 6, *perek* 5–6, pp. 83–86. Scholem states the *Schekhina* is the "Beautiful One upon whom no one may look" as is written in the Zohar. But the Aramaic

text can be interpreted as saying that she is the Beautiful One who *has no eyes*. If one accepts this interpretation, it is especially applicable to Luria since he teaches that the *Schekhina* can not retain the light's own impression (i.e., without retina) and gives while living in darkness to those who live within her sovereignty. For this reason she is poor compared to the other *sefiroth*. See Scholem in *Die Jüdische Mystik* (Zürich: Suhrkamp, 1957), p. 435. Cf. Genesis 29:17, "And Leah's eyes were weak. However, Rachel was of beautiful form and fair to look upon."

[22] Scholem, *Die Jüdische Mystik*, p. 236.

[23] See Idel in *Kabbalah: New Perspectives*: ". . . . the entire Zoharic and Lurianic superstructure is viewed, not only comprised in man-but *only* in man," p. 152. Also see Bar-Lev in *Song of the Soul*, pp. 170–182.

[24] See Daniel Matt, *The Essential Kabbalah*, (New York: Harper-Collins: 1995), pp. 167–169 and Bar-Lev in *Song of the Soul*, especially *akudim*, p. 198ff. These lights are undifferentiated and form the background of worlds with which we have no connection. They deal only with the future. Sefirothic worlds, on the other hand, form the present and are emanated by Adam Kadmon: *atsiluth* (emanation), *beriah* (creation), *jezira* (forming) and *asiyah* (making). These worlds are fully differentiated.

[25] See Vital, *Peri 'ets hayim Shaar 11, perek 4*, pp. 150–151.

[26] See Vital, *Peri 'ets hayim Hekha* l II. *Nekudim*. Gate 11. *Shaar ha-melakhim*. *Perek* 5, p. 153. Also see Isaiah Tishby, "Gnostic Doctrines in Sixteenth Century Jewish Mysticism," *Journal of Jewish Studies* 6 (1955), p. 147. See Matt, *The Essential Kabbalah*, pp. 15–16.

[27] See David Biale "Sixteenth Century Jewish Mysticism" in *An Introduction to Medieval Mystics in Europe*, p. 324 and Bar-Lev in *Song of the Soul*, p. 217. Bar-Lev explains that God intended that *sefiroth* would be free of one guiding power such that they ". . . wanted to operate independently of the others." It was at this stage that the origin of evil was actualized, the vessels broke, and free will was pre-created.

[28] See Vital, *Peri 'ets hayim*, *Hekhal* II. *Nekudim*, Gate 8. *Derushe nekudot*, *Perek* 4, p. 113.

[29] "*Tikkun*—the repair of the blemish, the event of making whole. . . . The moment of *tikkun* constitutes the point of denouement in a story; it echoes the pattern of cosmic history as grasped by Lurianic Kabbala, a pattern which culminates in *tikkun* which in its larger ramifications includes redemption, the end of Israel's exile, and a restored wholeness encompassing all the worlds. . . . The antithesis of *tikkun* is exile, the greater exile which marks all of existence and which is symbolized by Israel's historical experience of the exile." Aryeh Wineman, "The Dialectic of Tikkun in the Legends of the Ari," in *Prooftexts: A Journal of Jewish Literary History*, vol. 5, no. 1

(Baltimore: Johns Hopkins University Press, 1985), pp. 38–39. See also Franck, *Die Kabbala*, pp. 149–150.

[30] Vital, *Peri 'ets hayim, Hekhal 2. Nekudim. Shaar 11. ha-Melakhim. Perek 5*, p. 150. *Sefer Mavo shearim*, v. 5, p. 3. See also Dan, "Ethics in Sixteenth-Century Safed," pp. 95–96 and Klein, *Kabbalah of Creation*, pp. 69–70.

[31] See Isaiah Tishby, "Gnostic Doctrines in Sixteenth Century Jewish Mysticism," *Journal of Jewish Studies* 6 (1955), p. 147.

[32] Scholem describes how good is embedded in evil and that kabbalists explain this idea in the image of a realm. ". . . into which both of these emanations are mixed and are especially important regarding the origin of souls. According to a mystical interpretation of the Merkaba-vision of Ezechiel, in which the prophet observes the majesty of God behind veils of clouds, fire and radiance, the vision of a *kelipath ha-noga*, a world of shells arose, which is really the world of Lucifer, a world, which indeed belongs to that of shells, and consequently to that of evil, into which, however, a radiance from the world of *sefiroth* intervenes and permeates universally, so that the realms of good and evil appear grotesquely mixed." Trans. author of this article. The teaching of *kelipath ha-noga* can be found in the conclusion of Vital's *Ets Hayim*. See Gershom Scholem, *Von der mystischen Gestalt der Gottheit* (Zurich: Rhein-Verlag, 1962), pp. 72–73.

[33] See Pinchas Giller, *Reading the Zohar* (Oxford: Oxford University Press, 2001), pp. 105–117 and Scholem, *Die Jüdische Mystik*, pp. 290–310.

[34] See Vital, *Peri 'ets hayim, Hekhal VII. Atsilut, Beriah, Yetsirah, Asiyah*, Gate 48, *ha-Kelipot*, p. 370. "*Ze'ir Anpin* and *Nukva* are the names of God. . . . They are spirit and their birth is hidden in the secret of divine consciousness. . . . *Ze'ir Anpin* develops with great majesty and the *Nukva* in him are the sons of the ten full sefirot." See *Hekhal* 1. Adam kadmon. *Shaar* (Gate) 5. *Teamim, Nekudot, Tagim, Otiyot. Perek* 6, p. 73.

[35] Vital, *Peri 'ets hayim, Hekhal VI. Shaar* 36. *Perek* 2, p. 188.

[36] C. G. Jung, *Wandlungen und Symbole der Libido*, pp. 123–124; 113.

[37] *Shaar ha-pesukim*, v. 8 (of *Peri Ets hayim*), *Parashat Bereshit*, pp. 12–13.

[38] Ibid.

[39] *Shaar ha-Mitsvot*, v. 9, p. 112.

[40] C. G. Jung, *Psychologie und Religion* (Munchen: Deutscher Taschenbuch Verlag, 1990), p. 60. See also *Aurea hora*, a pseudo-Thomas Aquinas treatise of the 13th century.

[41] See Vital, *Peri 'ets hayim, Shaar* 39, pp. 227–228.

[42] See Dan, "Ethics in Sixteenth-Century Safed," p. 100.

[43] *Shaar ha-pesukim*, v. 8., p. 4 and p. 6. Commentary on Genesis 2:17. Also see See Gershom Scholem, *Zur Kabbala und ihrer Symbolik* (Frankfurt: Surhkamp, 1998), pp. 144–145. "Every transgression below causes one above. . . . *Ze'ir Anpin* desires the *Nukva*. . . . And as he desired her in the world of *Aziluth*, she went into exile below in creation." See Vital, *Peri 'ets hayim Hekhal* VII, 8, gate 49, p. 380. There are at least five accounts of the fall of Adam in the Lurianic texts. Accounts range from earthly, to sefirothic, and finally to parzufic. The preceding was the parzufic account.

[44] "The Holy One said to Adam that he was not of the world of *Asiyah* and he should not eat from the tree of knowledge. When he ate from it, he fell and became lessened. The tree of knowledge is in *Malkhut*, which is *Asiyah*." And: "*Adam ha-Rishon* made the *Shekhinah* depart to the first heavens . . ." And further: "Because of the sin of *Adam ha-Rishon*, Knowledge descended between his two shoulders. . . . the *gevurot* [*din*] descended first. . . . and the *gevurot* were not sweetened by the *hasadim*. . . . And this is one defect. . . . and the second defect is that only *gevurot* spread in the body of *Ze'ir Anpin* without the spread of the *hasidim* [to mitigate the harsh *gevurot* in him]. . . . And exterior ones grasp in them." See Vital, *Peri 'ets hayim*, *Hekhal* VI, *Shaar* 39, p. 228; *Hekhal* VI, *Shaar* 36, p. 187; *Hekhal* VII, 9, gate 50, p. 395.

[45] See *Shaar ha-pesukim*, v. 8, p. 7.

[46] See note 4 in *sefer ha-likutm. Parashat bereshit* 3. *anaf* 2.

[47] See I. Tishby, *Torat ha-ra` veha-Kelipah be-Kabalat ha-Ari*, trans. Nathan Snyder (Jerusalem: Hebrew University, 1942), p. 115.

[48] Hayyim Vital, 1542. *Sha'ar ha-kelalim*. English & Hebrew, trans. Eliahu Klein: *Kabbalah of Creation*, p. 46.

[49] See Giller, *Reading the Zohar*, pp. 152–153.

[50] See Scholem, *Die Jüdische Mystik*, p. 303.

[51] See Klein, *Kabbalah of Creation*, p. 132.

[52] See Scholem, *Judaica I* (Frankfurt: Suhrkamp, 1963), p. 143.

[53] See Scholem, *Die Jüdische Mystik*, p. 301.

Legend

Each work in Hebrew is cited using the following abbreviations:

Peri Ez Hayyim—PEH
Sefer Ets hayim—SEH
Sefer ha-kavanot—SSh-k
Sefer ha-likutim—Sh-l
Sefer ha-mitsvot—SSh-m
Sefer ha-pesukim—SSh-p
Sefer mavo shearim—Sms
Sefer ha-tselem—SSh-t-Chapter 26 of Ez chayim
Sefer Maamare Rashbi—SSMR
Sefer ha-gilgulim—SSh-g
Shaare kedushah—SSk
Hekhal—He
Shaar—Sh

Vital, Hayyim ben Joseph. 1542, *Peri 'ets hayim.* Tel Aviv, 1965, 15 vols.

Shaare kedushah. Derekh Hayim. *Sefer ha-hezyonot (likutim),* Bene-Berak, 1966.

Sefer ha-gilgulim : derush ha-neshamot veha-gilgul veha-ibur veha-yevum. Przemysl, 1875.

Sefer ha-likutim : al Torah, Neviim, Ketuvim. Yerushalayim, 1980.

The Kings of Edom

1. PEH. He 2, Sh 9.

2. PEH. He 2, Sh 8.

3. PEH. He 2, Sh 8.

4. PEH. He 7, Sh 49.

5–17. PEH. He 2, Sh 9.

18. PEH. He 2, Sh 11.

19. PEH. He 2, Sh 11.

20. PEH. He 2, Sh 8.

21–24. PEH. He 2, Sh 11.

25–26. PEH. He 2, Sh 9.

27–34. PEH. He 2, Sh 8.

35. PEH. He 2, Sh 11.

36. PEH. He 7, Sh 49.

37. PEH. He 6, Sh 35.

38–44. PEH. He 2, Sh 8.

45. PEH. He 7, Sh 42.

46. Sh-l., p. 464.

47–48. PEH. He 6, Sh 39.

49–54. PEH. He 7, Sh 50.

55–57. PEH. He 7, Sh 42.

58–59. PEH. He 2, Sh 8.

60–68. PEH. He 7, Sh 48.

69. PEH. He 7, Sh 42.

70. PEH. He 2, Sh 8.

71. PEH. He 2, Sh 11.

72. PEH. He 2, Sh 9.

73–74. PEH. He 1, Sh 6.

75. SEH. Sh 39.

76–79. PEH. He 2, Sh 9.

80–86. PEH. He 7, Sh 49.

87–98. PEH. He 2, Sh 9.

99. PEH. He 7, Sh 49.

100. PEH. He 6, Sh 49.

101–102. SSMR. v. 7.

103–106. PEH. He 7, Sh 48.

107. SSh-g. v.2.

108–109. Sms. Sh2, v. 5.

110. PEH. He 6, Sh 34.

Divine Rebirth

1–10. PEH. Hekhal I, Shaar 1.

11. SSh-ms. Hekhal 1, Perek 2.

12–26. PEH. Hekhal I, Shaar1.

27–31. PEH. He 2, Sh 11.

32–46. PEH. He 1, Sh 1.

47–59. PEH. He 2, Sh11.

60–73. PEH. He1, Sh 1.

74. Yerid ha -sefarim, 758 (1998). 10 v., 103–102. Sefer Tikune Zohar. Introduction.

75–88. PEH. He 1, Sh 1.

89–102. PEH. He 1, Sh 5.

103–112. PEH. He 1, Sh 7.

113–116. PEH. He 7, Sh 42.

117–123. Commentary on the Torah / (by) Ramban

(Nachmanides); tr. Rabbi Dr. Charles B. Chavel.
New York: Shilo Pub. House (1971–1976), v. 1.

124–165. PEH. He 7, Sh 42.

166–168. PEH. He 1, Sh 1.

169–178. PEH. He 7, Sh 42.

179–215. PEH. He 5, Sh 26.

216–226. PEH. He 1, Sh 1.

227–230. PEH. He 1, Sh 7.

231–236. PEH. He 1, Sh 1.

237. PEH. He 1, Sh 5.

238. PEH. He 1, Sh 1.

239–255. PEH. He 7, Sh 47.

256–261. PEH. He 7, Sh 48.

262. SSh-ms. Sh 2, Helek 2.

263–264. Sms. v. 5, p. 28.

265. SSh-p.

266. SSh-m. v. 9.

267–268. SSk. helik 3, Sh 2.

269. note 3 Mavo shearim. Shaar 1 perek 2. 2a.

270. Sms. v. 5, perek 3.

271. SEH. v. 1, p. 254.

272. Sms. v. 5, Sh 6.

273. SEH. v. 1, p. 4. Shaar ha-kelalim. Perek 2. Seder ha-Tikun.

274. Sms. v. 5.

275. SEH. v. 1, p. 82. Shaar Akudim. Perek 5.

276–278. PEH. Sh 50, Perek 1.

279. SSk. He 3, Sh 2.

280. SSh-m. v. 9.

Adam among the Worlds

1. SSk. Sh 2, p. 96.

2. SSk. Sh2, p. 96.

3. SSk. Sh2, p. 96.

4. Sh-l. parashat noah 8. Anaf 3.

5. SSh-p. v. 8, p. 13.

6. SSh-p. v. 8, p. 13.

7. SSh-m. v. 9.

8. SSh-p. v. 8, p. 225.

9. SSh-t. Ch 26, Perek 1.

10. PEH. He 7, Sh 47.

11. PEH. He 6, Sh 39.

12. PEH. He 6 Sh 39.

13. PEH. He 6, Sh 47.

14. See Note 2 in parashat va-yishlah 22 Anaf 2.

15. PEH. He 7, Sh 48.

16. PEH. He 7, Sh 48.

17. PEH. He 7, Sh 48.

18. PEH. He 7, Sh 47.

19. PEH. He 7, Sh 47.

20. PEH. He 7, Sh 43.

21. PEH. He 7, Sh 43.

22. PEH. He 7, Sh 43.

23. PEH. He 7, Sh 43.

24. PEH. He 7, Sh 43.

25. PEH. He 7, Sh 43.

26. PEH. He 7, Sh 42.

27. PEH. He 7I, Sh 42.

28. PEH. He 7, Sh 42.

29. PEH. He 7, Sh 42.

30. PEH. He 7, Sh 42.

31. PEH. He 7, p. 310.

32. PEH. He 7, Sh 42.

33. PEH. He 7, Sh 42.

34. PEH. He 7, Sh 42.

35. SSk. Sh 2, p. 94.

36. SSk. Sh 2, pp. 95–96.

37. SSk. Sh 2, p. 90.

38. SSk. Sh 2, p. 90.

39. SSk. Sh 2, p. 90.

40. SSk. Sh 2, p. 92.

41. SSk. Sh 2, p. 92.

42. SSk. Sh 2, p. 92.

43. SSk. Sh 2, p. 92.

44. SSk. Sh 2, p. 92.

45. SSk. Sh 2, p. 92.

46. PEH. He 6, Sh 34.

47. PEH. He 6, Sh 34.

48. PEH. He 6, Sh 43.

49. PEH. He 6, Sh 43.

50. PEH. He 6, Sh 43.

51. PEH. He 7, Sh 43.

52. PEH. He 7, Sh 43.

53. PEH. He 7, Sh 43.

54. PEH. He 7, Sh 43.

55. PEH. He 7, Sh 43.
56. PEH. He 7, Sh 43.
57. PEH. He 7, Sh 43.
58. PEH. He 7, Sh 43.
59. PEH. He 7, Sh 48.
60. PEH. He 7, Sh 48.
61. PEH. He 7, Sh 48.
62. PEH. He 7, Sh 50.
63. PEH. He 7, Sh 48.
64. PEH. He 7, Sh 48.
65. PEH. He 7, Sh 48.
66. PEH. He 7, Sh 49.
67. PEH. He 7, Sh 49.
68. PEH. He 7, Sh 48.
69. PEH. He 7, Sh 48.
70. PEH. He 7, Sh 49.
71. PEH. He 7, Sh 48.
72. PEH. He 7, Sh 48.
73. PEH. He 7, Sh 48.
74. PEH. He 7, Sh 48.
75. PEH. He 7, Sh 48.
76. PEH. He 7, Sh 49.
77. PEH. He 7, Sh 49.
78. PEH. He 7, Sh 49.
79. PEH. He 7, Sh 49.
80. PEH. He 7, Sh 49.
81. PEH. He 7, Sh 49.
82. PEH. He 7, Sh 49.

83. PEH. He 7, Sh 49.

84. PEH. He 7, Sh 43.

85. PEH. He 7, Sh 48.

86. PEH. He 7, Sh 48.

87. PEH. He 7, Sh 48.

88. PEH. He 7, Sh 50.

89. PEH. He 7, Sh 50.

90. PEH. He 7, Sh 50.

91. PEH. He 7, Sh 50.

92. PEH. He 7, Sh 50.

93. PEH. He 7, Sh 50.

94. PEH. He 7, Sh 50.

95. PEH. He 7, Sh 50.

96. PEH. He 7, Sh 50.

97. PEH. Hel 7, Sh 50.

98. PEH. He 7, Sh 50.

99. SSMR. p. 63.

100. SSMR. p. 63.

101. SSMR. p. 63.

102. SSMR. p. 63.

103. SSk. Sh 2, p. 95.

104. SSk. Sh 2, p. 88.

105. SSk. Sh 2, p. 89.

106. SSk. Sh 2, p. 89.

107. SSk. Sh 2, p. 89.

108. SSk. Sh 2, p. 94.

109. PEH. He 6, Sh 34.

110. PEH. He 6, Sh 34.

111. PEH. Hekhal 6, Sh 34.

112. PEH. He 6, Sh 34.

113. PEH. He 6, Sh 34.

114. PEH. He 6, Sh 34.

115. PEH. He 6, Sh 35.

116. PEH. He 6, Sh 38.

117. PEH. He 6, Sh 38.

118. PEH. He 6, Sh 38.

119. PEH. He 6, Sh 39.

120. SSh-g. v. 2, p. 35a.

121. SSh-g. v. 2, p. 35a.

122. SSh-g. v. 2, p. 35a.

123. PEH. He 6, Sh 38.

124. PEH. He 6, Sh 38.

125. PEH. He 6, Sh 38.

126. PEH. He 6, Sh 38.

127. PEH. He 6, Sh 36.

128. PEH. He 6, Sh 47.

129. SSk. Helek 3, Sh 2, pp. 91–92.

130. SSk. Helek 1. Sh 1, p. 13–14.

131. SSk. Helek 3, Sh 5, p. 101.

132. PEH. Sh 49, v. 2, pp. 386–387.

Benedictions of the Soul

1. SSh-p. v. 8.
2. SSh-p. v. 8.

3. SSh-p. v. 8.

4. SSh-p. v. 8.

5. SSh-p. v. 8, (note. Talmud. Tractate Avodah zarah. 9a. Talmud Eser Sefirot. Lesson 8 from Letter 76 to Letter 88.)

6. SSh-p. v. 8.

7. SSh-p. v. 8.

8. SSh-p. v. 8.

9. SSh-p. v. 8.

10. SSh-k. v. 10, (Lecture 2), p. 303.

11. SSMR. v. 7, p. 166.

12. PEH. Shaar 39, v. 2, p. 222.

13. SSMR. v. 7.

14. SSMR. v. 7.

15. SSMR. v. 7.

16. SSMR. v. 7.

17. SSMR. v. 7.

18. SSMR. v. 7.

19. SSMR. v. 7.

20. SSh-m. v. 9.

21. SSh-m. v. 9.

22. SSh-m. v. 9.

23. SSh-m. v. 9.

24. SSh-m. v. 9.

25. SSh-m. v. 9.

26. SSh-m. v. 9.

27. SSh-m. v. 9.

28. SSh-m. v. 9.

29. SSh-m. v. 9.

30. SSh-p. v. 8.

31. SSh-p. v. 8.

32. SSh-p. v. 8.

33. SSh-p. v. 8.

34. SSh-p. v. 8.

35. SSh-k. v. 10.

36. SSh-k. v. 10.

37. SSh-k. v. 10.

38. SSh-k. v. 10.

39. SSh-k. v. 10.

40. SSh-k. v. 10.

41. SSh-k. v. 10.

42. SSh-k. v. 10.

43. SSh-k. v. 10.

44. SSh-k. v. 10.

45. SSh-k. v. 10.

46. SSh-k. v. 10.

47. SSh-k. v. 10.

48. SSh-k. v. 10.

49. SSh-k. v. 10.

50. SSh-k. v. 10.

51. SSh-k. v. 10.

52. SSh-k. v. 10.

53. SSh-k. v. 10.

54. PEH. Shaar ha-kelalim. Perek 1, v. 1.

55. SSh-m. v. 9.

56. SSh-m. v. 9.

57. SSh-m. v. 9.

58. SSh-m. v. 9.

59. SSh-m. v. 9.

60. SSh-k. v. 10.

61. PEH. He VII, Sh 50.

62. SSh-k. v. 10.

63. SSh-k. v. 10.

64. SSh-k. v. 10.

65. SSh-m. v. 9.

66. SSh-m. v. 9.

67. SSh-m. v. 9.

68. SSh-m. v. 9.

69. SSh-m. v. 9.

70. SSh-m. v. 9.

71. SSh-m. v. 9.

72. SSh-m. v. 9.

73. SSh-m. v. 9.

74. SSh-m. v. 9.

75. PEH. He VI, Sh 34.

76. PEH. Sh ha-kelalim. Perek 1. v. 1.

77. SSh-k. v. 10.

78. SSh-p. v. 8 (commentary to Parashat Shemot of Exodus 1-6:1), p. 101.

79. SSh-m. v. 9.

80. SSMR. Parashat Va-yakhel. v. 7, pp. 157–158.

81. SSh-m. v. 9.

82–85. Sms. Sh 2, helek 2, perek 2, v. 5. [Note: PEH. Shaar ha-melakhim. Perek 6; Sh ha kdamot, p 228; in PEH with Panim masbirot, Anaf 11 and 12.]

About the Author

James Dunn is professor of foreign languages at San Antonio College in San Antonio, Texas. His private and most passionate work for over 25 years has been Judaic mysticism and Jungian depth psychology. Through many years of research, he found those teachings that unlock the worlds of the subconscious mind through revelations from the secrets of Kaballah, translated from the original passages of Hebrew—*Window of the Soul*. James Dunn is a distinguished languages educator and retired intelligence officer. He served in the Pentagon, NSA and Europe, and was decorated many times for distinguished military service. He is a member of Mensa, has been published in *Who's Who in American Education, Who's Who in America,* and *Who's Who among America's Teachers.*